D1715118

THE ECONOMIC VALUE
OF
EDUCATION

THE ECONOMIC VALUE
OF
EDUCATION

THEODORE W. SCHULTZ

COLUMBIA UNIVERSITY PRESS

New York and London

FOREWORD

This monograph is one of a series of three dealing with the economics of health, education, and welfare. In commissioning these volumes, the Ford Foundation was influenced by the fact that expenditures in these three fields are in excess of $100 billion annually, that they are among the most important and sensitive areas of the entire economy, and that communication between economists and those making policy and operating decisions in these areas has been infrequent and irregular.

In the last few years an important literature on the economics of education has begun to develop. Professor Theodore W. Schultz has been one of the leading contributors to this literature, and he was, therefore, a logical choice to undertake a review of past work and to suggest future research opportunities. It is hoped that this volume will prove of value to school administrators, members of school boards, university trustees and administrators, legislators charged with determining the amount and direction of flow of public funds to education, and others with similar interests and responsibilities. This book will certainly not solve all their problems nor answer all their questions, but it may open up new lines of thought and provide an introduction to the light that economics can throw on problems of education. Professor Schultz's colleagues within the economics profession will appreciate his succinct and knowledgeable review of the literature and may find themselves stimulated to make their own research contributions to this vital area of public policy.

The other two monographs in the series are *The Economics of Welfare Policies* by Dr. Margaret S. Gordon of the University of California (Berkeley) and *The Economics of Health* by Professor Herbert Klarman of the Johns Hopkins University. All three authors have been free to develop and interpret the materials in their chosen field according to their own judgment; the views expressed are, of course, their own. The Ford Foundation is grateful to them for the time and care that they have devoted to this important task.

Henry H. Villard, *Director*
Program in Economic Development
and Administration

June, 1963
New York City

PREFACE

There is a lively and rapidly growing interest in the economic value of education. I see it especially in economics although there are also some signs of it in education. It is a new field in the sense that several recent studies are based on a new approach. These studies also have raised some questions that are as yet unsettled. Knowing this, when Victor R. Fuchs invited me to prepare this essay, I accepted with misgivings. Nor has my task been made any the less difficult by developments in this field since I started this essay. A number of important studies have become available,[1] a flock of conferences on "Economics and Education" have been held,[2] and a lively debate has gotten underway on some of the underlying issues.

[1] The principal ones that bear directly on the aims of this essay are the papers that appeared in the Supplement, "Investment in Human Beings," *Journal of Political Economy*, 70 (October, 1962). This Supplement was sponsored and supported by the National Bureau of Economic Research and copies of it are available from the NBER, $1.25. Fritz Machlup's book, *The Production and Distribution of Knowledge in the United States*, Princeton University Press, 1962, $7.50, appeared late in 1962. I have written a review of it which will appear in the *American Economic Review*. Gary S. Becker's study, *Investment in Education*, has been completed. It is being published as a study of the National Bureau of Economic Research. I have had the privilege of reading a completed draft of this excellent study. As I write, Lee R. Martin's paper, "Research Needed on the Contribution of Human, Social and Community Capital to Economic Growth," *Journal of Farm Economics*, 45 (February, 1963), has just appeared.

[2] The OECD held a conference in Washington D.C., October, 1961, on Economic Growth and Investment in Education. UNESCO, along with other international agencies, concentrated on Education and Economic Development in Latin America, meeting in Santiago, Chile, March, 1962. The Agricultural Policy Institute of North Carolina State College and the Southern Regional Education Board held a conference on Educational Needs for Economic Development of the South at Asheville, N. C.,

My own interest in this field took shape during 1956–57 while I was a fellow at the Center for Advanced Study of the Behavioral Sciences.[3] I had been puzzled by the fact that the concepts that I was using to measure capital and labor were close to being empty in explaining the increases in production that occurred over time. During the year at the Center, I began to see that the productive essences of what I was identifying as capital and labor were not constant but were being improved over time and that these improvements were being left out in what I was measuring as capital and labor. It became clear to me also that in the United States many people are investing heavily in themselves as human agents, that these investments in man are having a pervasive influence upon economic growth, and that the key investment in human capital is education.

I am aware that an essay on the economic value of education will seem presumptuous to many school people and to some economists. Those who value schooling highly, which includes most of those who are a part of the educational establishment, are likely to look upon an effort such as this as an intrusion which can only debase the cultural purposes of education. In their view education lies beyond the economic calculus, because they believe that education is much more than a matter of costs and returns. To speak of schooling as an investment is to imply that it is something material. The notion of "efficiency" is a red flag in most school circles and often for good reasons when it is implied that an efficiency expert from business or a foundation is qualified to evaluate teaching and learning.

June, 1962. The Social Sciences Research Council sponsored a conference on Education and Economic Development at the University of Chicago, April, 1963. OECD reentered this field with a Study Group in Economics of Education addressing itself to "The Residual Factor and Economic Growth," meeting in Paris, May, 1963. Then, in late August and early September, 1963, the International Economic Association will hold a conference at Menthon St. Bernard, Lac d'Annecy, France, on The Economics of Education.

[3]The Center at that time was supported wholly by the Ford Foundation and thus indirectly I am obligated to the Foundation for the generous fellowship awarded to me that year. My obligation to Ralph Tyler, director of the Center, is large and direct.

But on the latter issue I may be spared because I have little to say about "efficiency" within schools. It will become clear as I proceed that there are other important economic questions related to schooling which I propose to investigate. When these questions have been clarified, I am sure it will allay the apprehensions of school people. It will become clear that there are important economic dimensions to education that have not been fully recognized and that these dimensions augment substantially the value traditionally attributed to schooling and to on-campus research.

The debate that is underway aimed at issues in this field is often far off the mark. One such is the long overdue debate on the large "residual" in economic growth. The critical question to be resolved in this connection goes far beyond the economic value of education. If it is a real residual, as is assumed in so much of this debate, then obviously the following question matters: What logical basis is there for attributing this residual to any factor? But if the observed residual is predominantly a consequence of the specification and measurement of output and input, then the question would be: What is being omitted in the growth models that "attribute" so much of the increase in output to a "residual"? It is my contention that such omissions are both real and important. Many economists have been playing a game called economic growth which has made them ever more adept at disembodying the two primary inputs. Both labor and nonhuman capital have become essentially empty shells and thus it should not come as a surprise that this game has not explained growth. But it has succeeded in removing the increases in the productive essence of the real factors of production that have accounted for much of our growth during recent decades. What is happening in the economy is that an array of new factors of production is being introduced and the quality of old factors is being improved, and the growth game has been to conceal the additional productive services from these sources under so-called "technological change." The implication here is that the large "residual" is simply a bias of the analytical approach most economists have been using. To correct this bias it will be necessary to develop an all-inclusive concept of the factors of production including the economic productivity of education.

In the current debate another type of question has arisen that also is off the mark. Let me state this question. Is it permissible to extend the concept of capital to man, specifically to include the acquired skills and knowledge of the human agent that augment his economic productivity? That an economist should raise this question is odd, for in economics it has long been known that people are an important part of the wealth of nations. The philosopher-economist, Adam Smith, boldly included all of the acquired and useful abilities of all the inhabitants of a country as a part of capital, and he gave the right reasons for doing so. H. von Thunen also saw this issue clearly as did others. Irving Fisher more than a half a century ago laid the analytical foundation for an all-inclusive concept of capital including both man and material objects. But Fisher's conception of capital unfortunately has long been neglected. Instead, the concept of capital has become ever more identified with goods—reproducible goods. Surely one of the major reasons for the widely held popular belief that economics is materialistic is the over-commitment on the part of economists to a partial concept of capital restricted to material objects. The failure to include the acquired abilities of man that augment his economic productivity as a form of capital, as a produced means of production, as a product of investment, has fostered the retention of the patently wrong notion that labor is capital-free and that it is only the number of manhours worked that matters. But as I have pointed out elsewhere, laborers have become capitalists in the sense that they have acquired much knowledge and many skills that have economic value. Clearly what is needed in this connection is an all-inclusive concept of capital.

This essay rests on the proposition that people enhance their capabilities as producers and as consumers by investing in themselves and that schooling is the largest investment in human capital. This proposition implies that most of the economic capabilities of people are not given at birth or at the time when children enter upon their schooling. These acquired capabilities are anything but trivial. They are of a magnitude to alter radically the usual measures of the amount of savings and of capital formation that is taking place. They also alter the structure of wages and salaries and the amount of earnings from work relative to the amount of income from property. There are long-standing puzzles about economic growth, changes in the structure of wages and salaries, and changes in the personal distribution of income that can be substantially resolved by taking account of investment in human capital.

The economic value of education depends predominantly on the demand for and the supply of schooling approached as an investment. A number of challenging studies are under way concentrating on the economic components of education. Although the findings are still subject to revision, as methods of analysis and data are improved, it already is worthwhile to take stock. By examining these findings and the basis on which they rest, I hope to clarify a number of major unsettled questions that await further economic analysis. The clarification of these questions is the central aim of this essay. One might have thought that at least the costs of schooling would be known. Not only are they reckoned in ways that make it hard to interpret them; but, what is much more serious, a large class of these costs is hidden, and until very recently nothing had been done to discover the amount of these hidden costs and who bears them. It turns out that when they are brought into the picture, parts of the educational scene that always appear blurred become clear.

Yet to determine costs is like meeting a gentle breeze compared to standing up against a violent wind when one seeks an answer to: "What are the values of education?" But real progress has been made. When viewed as economic attributes, the returns consist of satisfactions, a consumer component, and of acquired capabilities, a producer component.

A word on what is omitted in this essay. Public finance of education belongs here but it is not included because the literature is large, self-contained, and readily available. There are a a number of very useful studies of human resources concentrating on high level manpower required for economic growth and on the demand for and supply of particular skills. These are also omitted, and for the same reason. Although economic analysis can make real contributions in finding ways to improve the management of schools, this area of analysis is still so uncharted that it could not be treated adequately in this essay. No attempt is made to present the policy implications of what is covered or to develop a critique of existing policy related to education.

I have accumulated many obligations in preparing this essay. I drew heavily on early drafts of the papers of Gary S. Becker, Edward F. Denison, Jacob Mincer, and Burton A. Weisbrod that have now appeared in the *Journal of Political Economy* Supplement, "Investment in Human Beings." I also was privileged in seeing the study by Gary S. Becker on *Investment in Education* and the paper by W. Lee Hansen on "Total and Private Rates of Return to Investment in Schooling," in draft before they were completed. Mary Jean Bowman, Victor R. Fuchs, and W. Lee Hansen read a draft of this essay and I accepted nearly all of their valuable criticisms. Sherwin S. Rosen assisted me in preparing the bibliography. My wife, Esther Werth Schultz, not only caught errors as I wrote but convinced me on many points that what I thought was clear still lacked clarity. I am also obligated to Josephine Guemple for her endless patience and fine work in typing the manuscript. During the last three years in pursuing my studies in this field I drew upon a generous grant from the Fund for the Advancement of Education of the Ford Foundation, which I gratefully acknowledge.

Theodore W. Schultz

The University of Chicago
June, 1963

CONTENTS

CONTENTS

THE ECONOMIC VALUE
OF
EDUCATION

I. ECONOMIC COMPONENTS
OF EDUCATION

My aim is to bring economic analysis to bear on education. Until recently, judging by what economists have done in this area, one might infer that the tools of economists were not useful in studying education, or perhaps that the costs and economic value of education were not important enough to warrant their attention. The early masters provided no systematic treatment of education when they developed the analytical core and staked out the boundaries of economics. Neither the satisfactions that people derive from schooling nor the investment attributes which enhance productivity and earnings of workers were investigated. The reasons for this neglect of the economics of education are shrouded in the *Weltanschauung* of the time, about which there are some speculations [70, 191].*

Upon reflection the economist who contemplates entering here may feel reluctant. He is, as a rule, an educator and thus mindful that he has a vested interest in education which could cast a doubt on his impartiality. Education is intimately a part of the culture of the community which the economist shares, and this too creates a presumption that he cannot be wholly objective. No doubt there are more risks here than in the old plots that have long been cultivated by economists.

In asking questions pertaining to education and in classifying the components to be studied, an economist is guided by theory. But theory, and economic theory is no exception, always abstracts from particular attributes of the activities that are being investigated. The fact that there are some attributes of

---

* Numbers in square brackets refer to the Selected Bibliography, pp. 71–89.

education that can be treated by economics does not mean
that they are necessarily important. Nor does it imply that those
which economic theory "puts aside" are unimportant. Surely the
findings that emerge out of the work of economists in this area
are by no means all of the educational story. Yet this fact is not
inconsistent with the belief that economic knowledge about education is both real and relevant in making private and public decisions with regard to education.

What, then, are the questions that matter when it comes to the
economics of education? How are the economic components of
education to be classified? As a rule, too little thought is given
to these issues, judging by what some economists do. It has
been fashionable to produce models without much thought as to
whether the question which a particular model might serve to
answer really matters and, also, without sufficient regard to the
feasibility of getting back to the real world.

There is always the temptation to proceed promptly to the ultimate question about resource allocation, that is, how efficient
are we in our private and public decisions in the allocation of
resources entering into education? For a country in its entirety,
this question would require treating education at a very high
level of generality. The economic test of efficiency would be
that neither too many nor too few resources are being employed
to provide an optimum flow of educational services, which in
turn implies that the particular resources that are employed are
being used in the best combination to "produce" this flow of
educational services. At this level of generality, however, it is
exceedingly difficult to bring economic analysis to bear and not
lose contact with the substantive economic properties of the
cost components and, more especially, with the values of schooling. To most persons, moreover, resource allocation so broadly
conceived is likely to seem essentially hortatory.

I propose to begin with less comprehensive questions pertaining to education in order to get at issues that are analytically
more manageable at this stage of our knowledge. Inquiries di-
rected to these issues are giving us or will give us the essential pieces of knowledge that will permit us, as we advance, to

take on the more ultimate question. In the final analysis, however, it will be necessary to return to a comprehensive conception of resource allocation.

What Is Meant by Education?

Concepts of education, like those of freedom, bristle with difficulties. It is hard to define education because of what it connotes, which depends in no small measure upon the particular culture in which education occurs. Education is intimately bound to the culture of the community it serves, and for this reason what education means differs from one community to another. What all education has in common after allowance is made for these cultural differences is "teaching" and "learning." Thus, to educate means etymologically to educe or draw out of a person something potential and latent; it means to develop a person morally and mentally so that he is sensitive to individual and social choices and able to act on them; it means to fit him for a calling by systematic instruction; and it means to train, discipline, or form abilities, as, for example, to educate the taste of a person. The act or process of achieving one or more of these objectives is, as a first approximation, what education is about.

For some purposes "schooling" and "education" are interchangeable, but for other purposes a concept is required to represent the activities that are an integral part of the teaching and learning of students, and another concept to represent particular functions of the educational establishment. When it becomes necessary to make this distinction, I shall use *schooling* for the first and *education* for the second. Later in this study, I shall refer to a "year of schooling" as a first approximation of the amount of organized instruction that a person has received. Schooling is thus a concept applied to the educational services rendered by elementary and secondary schools and by institutions for higher learning, including the effort of students to learn. Organized education, however, is not only engaged in "producing" schooling but also in advancing knowledge through research, and for its own sake going beyond teaching or instruction that enters currently into schooling. The educational establishment is engaged in a number of activities which do not become an essential part of the achievement of students. Research, as already indicated, is one of the traditional functions of the educational establishment. Not so obvious, but important nevertheless, is the discovery and cultivation of potential talent. There is the special recruitment and instruction of teachers, reinforced by subtle indoctrination on behalf of the nonmaterial rewards of teaching. Thus, although schooling and education are often interchangeable terms, it will be necessary in this essay to distinguish between them.

I propose to treat education as a specialized set of activities, of which some are organized, as they are in schools, and some are essentially unorganized, as is education in the home. Machlup's [212] classification is instructive. In it he treats education as one of the activities that produces knowledge and he then proceeds to classify education into that which is done in the home, in the church, and in the armed services, education in firms consisting of on-the-job learning, and education in schools consisting mainly of elementary and secondary schools and institutions of higher education. Schools may be viewed as firms that specialize in "producing" schooling. The educational establishment, which includes all schools, may be viewed as an industry.

It is, of course, true that the educational establishment does not have some of the economic characteristics of a conventional industry. With a few unimportant exceptions, schools are not organized and administered for profit. The assets of educational institutions are not listed on any stock exchange. Students, or the families supporting them, do not as a rule pay all of the costs that are incurred in schooling. To the extent that schooling increases the future earnings of the student, it has the attributes of an investment. But the human capital thus created cannot be sold as can nonhuman capital. The contribution of most education is multidimensional, in serving at one and the same time social, political, and other purposes. These and other differences between the educational establishment and a conventional industry do not, however, preclude the application of economic analysis to education, although these differences must be taken into account by economists in their studies of education.

A new field of inquiry has its attractions. Education for the economists is such a field. In bringing economic analysis to bear, there are two components that matter. There also are issues which pertain to the manner in which education is organized and how effectively it uses resources. To gain perspective on these, let me begin with a sketch of them.

Two Basic Components

Whatever the benefits of schooling, costs really matter. They at once suffice to show that resources entering into schooling are not trivial. In the United States, for example, the annual costs of elementary, high school, and higher education exceed $30 billion. Costs also show that most of them are borne by students and their parents, notwithstanding the belief that schooling is virtually free because of public education. But it is most assuredly far from free for mature students because the earnings they forego while attending school are likely to exceed all of the other school costs incurred by them and for them. It would of course be possible to provide students with scholarships equal to the wages they could earn if they took jobs instead of continuing in school; this would shift the cost burden to someone else, but the underlying total costs to society would remain unchanged. I do not wish to indicate by this who should bear these and the other costs of schooling. My purpose here is simply to bring earnings foregone by students into the picture. The concept of foregone earnings as one of the costs of schooling is a key to a number of puzzles about education.

If earnings foregone were ignored, studies of lifetime earning differentials associated with levels of schooling would indicate an exceedingly high rate of return to what high school and college students in the United States have been paying for their schooling. Even when all of the public and private school expenditures are taken into account, this rate of return is still very high relative to the rate of return on alternative investment. When earnings foregone are included in the estimates of costs, estimates of the rate of return are cut by about 60 percent. Even so, the rate of return may be as high or appreciably higher than that on investment generally, but with the inclusion of earnings foregone in costs, the inordinate disparity in the rates of return is resolved.

Opportunity costs also provide a unified explanation of three other behaviors: *(a)* many talented children from low-income families do not continue their schooling beyond the age that is legally compulsory even though tuition is free or scholarships are available to cover tuition, *(b)* children from farm families attend school less regularly than do children from urban families, and *(c)* many children in low-income countries who complete the first few years of schooling drop out after that. In these three situations, earnings foregone appear to be a key because children can be called upon to do useful work and thus contribute to the meager family income.

In poor countries the costs of a (standard) year of elementary schooling decline as family incomes rise; whereas in high-income countries, the costs of a year of schooling at all levels increase markedly. Why should this be true? Why, for example, should the costs of a year of schooling in the United States rise over time relative to consumer prices and also relative to gross national product prices? In a section devoted to costs, estimates will be introduced which show that between 1930 and 1956 the costs of a year of elementary schooling rose about 60 percent relative to prices implicit in the gross national product and that for a year of high school about 90 percent.

While it is obvious that costs are a basic component in studying the economics of education, it is surprising how little has been done to develop appropriate concepts for this purpose and to identify and measure these costs.

What is the value of schooling? A babel of voices will respond to this query. It is moral, refines taste, and gives people real satisfactions. It is vocational, develops skills, increases earnings, and is an investment in man. Our task is to treat these and still other values of schooling in a framework of economic analysis.

But the moment it is suggested that the economic value of schooling is under consideration, there are many who protest, for they believe that placing a "price" on education is to debase it. "Whatever you do in studying education, do not apply an economic yardstick to its worth," expresses a deep-seated apprehension. This apprehension is groundless analytically. Although it is, of course, true that particular bits of economic knowledge are sometimes misused by those who have an axe to grind in shaping policy [69], there are no reasons for believing that education is more vulnerable in this respect than are other areas of endeavor.

But the belief that the values of schooling are beyond economics will undoubtedly persist at least until studies by economists demonstrate that this is not true. Meanwhile, it may be useful to examine an aspect of this issue; namely, the distinction that is often made between the "cultural" and "economic" attributes of schooling. Implicit in this distinction is a dichotomy which separates culture from economy, or the art of living viewed as cultural from the practice of earning a living, which is excluded from culture. Such a dichotomy, however, rests on a special and very narrow notion of culture. A general and comprehensive concept of culture does not exclude the consumption and production activities on which so much of economic analysis concentrates. How people earn their living is in general an integral part of a culture. Etymologically *cultura* in Latin means to till and cultivate, and where the growing of crops is undertaken it is agri*culture*. What matters here is that the manner by which people earn their living and the economy that serves them in this respect are an essential and important part of the culture of a people. So is science and technology in universities and throughout a modern economy. Then, too, even if all schooling were for moral purposes or for the refinement of taste, it is not free. In the United States, as already noted, it costs annually over $30 billion, and the well-being that is attained is presumably not unrelated to the amount spent. There is much grist here for the economists. I conclude this comment then by observing that it is misleading to treat an economy as if it were not a part of the culture of a community. Conversely, it is misleading to treat culture as if it had no economic implications; expenditures for moral purposes or refinement of taste are not beyond economic analysis.

The value of schooling is based on the proposition that schooling affects well-being favorably. To begin, let me assume that all of the benefits of schooling are *captured* by the student and, therefore, that none of the benefits of his schooling improve the well-being of his neighbors, of those who employ him and of his co-workers, and none are widely diffused in society. Schooling can contribute satisfactions either in the present (for example, immediate enjoyment of association with one's college fellows), or in the future (increased capacity to enjoy good books). When the benefits are in the future, schooling has the attributes of an investment. As an investment, it can affect either future consumption or future earnings. Thus, the consumption component of schooling is of two parts: schooling that serves present consumption and schooling as an investment to serve future consumption. The producer component of schooling is an investment in skills and knowledge which enhance future earnings, and thus it is like an investment in (other) producer goods.

The satisfaction that people obtain from schooling is the consumption component. It consists of values associated with education that are not as a rule vocational, occupational, or professional. Schooling to acquire abilities to increase future earnings is not consumption. When it is consumption, its value can be moral, or a refinement in taste, or some other source of satisfaction. To the extent that schooling is a consumer "good," it is predominantly an enduring component, even more enduring than most consumer durables. It is hard to find plausible examples of schooling that represent primarily present consumption. As an enduring consumer component, it is a source of future satisfactions which enhances future real income. But these satisfactions are not reckoned in *measured* national income.

Treating the expenditures for schooling as economists do other consumer expenditures opens the door for demand analysis to determine, among other things, both the price elasticity and the income elasticity of the demand for schooling. Although the prospects along these lines are slim, for reasons to be presented below, some useful knowledge can be won. While the relative price of educational services is not subject, as are raw materials and farm products, to major short period fluctuations, the real cost of schooling, hence its real price, rises more than the cost of living over long periods in countries in which real earnings of workers, including the salaries of teachers, rise relative to the price of other factors of production [20, Tables 13 and 28; 22; 130]. Accordingly, estimates of this price elasticity would be of some relevance in analyzing real decisions of people. The income elasticity of the demand for education is, however, more important because the real income per family has risen much over time in the United States and also in many other countries, and because the effects of income upon the demand for schooling appear to be large. There have been attempts to gauge this income elasticity, which suggests that it may be high, perhaps between 2.0[†] and 3.5 [19]. Studies restricted to school expenditures show much lower elasticities with respect to income: Fabricant [8] for 1942, 48 states and expenditures per capita for current operation obtains an elasticity of .78; Brazer [107] for 1953, 40 large cities, per capita operating expenditures .73; Hirsch [12] for 17 years selected from the period 1900-1958, United States daily total current expenditure plus debt service per pupil, 1.09; and, Shapiro [133] for 1950, for 48 states current expenditures per pupil, societal (where the above are all based on public expenditures), derived an elasticity of .94. There are, however, serious difficulties in making and interpreting these estimates. They cover only a part of all expenditures. Earnings foregone are not taken into account. Most of the education that satisfies consumer preferences has an enduring quality, and it is therefore not like food, but like a very long lasting consumer durable. The main difficulty, however, arises out of the fact that many educational

[†]Professor Margaret Reid has examined the expenditures of particular urban consumers, and her preliminary estimates tended to cluster around 2.0 for the income elasticity of the demand for education as revealed by these private expenditures for education.

expenditures have the properties of an investment in a producer capacity, and it is not correct, therefore, to treat this part as consumption. Nevertheless, there is, in education, a sizable component that argues for consumption and demand analysis.

Where schooling increases the future earnings of students, it is an investment. It is an investment in human capital in the form of abilities acquired in school. Investments in human capital are many and the amount has become large. Truly, it can be said, the productive capacity of labor is predominantly a *produced* means of production. We thus "make" ourselves and to this extent "human resources" are a consequence of investments among which schooling is of major importance.

From this it would appear that the analytical job with respect to the amount invested, the stock of such capital, the earnings attributed to it, and the rate of return to investment in schooling is straightforward. But appearances are misleading. As Becker shows, received theory of investment requires substantial reformulation to cope with investment in people [29]. The formal relations between earnings, rates of return, and the amount invested must first be determined before such theoretical relationships can be used as an analytical tool. Earning differentials are affected by such factors as age, sex, race, unemployment, inherited ability, informal education in the home, and city size along with schooling. Estimates of the amount invested in schooling to increase future earnings are affected in turn by the part of the costs of schooling that is attributed to present and future consumption. The rate of return will differ, also depending on whether we use the costs of schooling to students and to their parents or to them and others, so as to take account of the total factor costs of schooling.

For the purposes of this essay, it will suffice merely to say that studies of schooling which treat it as an investment are an important source of new knowledge about the economy. Investments in schooling are not trivial; quite the contrary, they are of a magnitude to alter radically the commonly accepted estimates of the amount of savings and capital formation that take place. Received propositions concerning the determinants of the structure of wages and salaries (relative earnings), the personal distribution of income, and the sources of economic growth will all require reformulation.

The investment in schooling has been large in the United States. The ''stock'' of such capital — formed by schooling — has been increasing at a rate that exceeds by a wide margin the rate at which the stock of material reproducible capital has been increasing. The rate of return to investment in schooling is as high or higher than it is to nonhuman capital, even when one attributes all of the costs of schooling to investment in earnings and, therefore, none of it to consumption. As a source of economic growth, the additional schooling of the labor force would appear to account for about one fifth of the rise in real national income in the United States between 1929 and 1957.

Earlier we imposed the assumption that all of the benefits of schooling are captured by the student. Weisbrod [78] examines a large set of benefits from education (he includes university research) other than future production returns that become a part of earnings. Clearly, schooling can benefit some persons other than the student. Other families benefit as neighbors and as taxpayers. There are some employment-related benefits which go to co-workers and to employers and some, as already noted, that are widely diffused in society.

Stability and Efficiency

The economic stability of the educational sector deserves to be mentioned. I know of no studies of the effects of recessions and recoveries (trade cycles) upon the educational establishment or of the effects of the apparent stability of this sector upon the rest of the economy. Education clearly is not one of the unstable sectors of the economy; on the contrary, it may have some dampening influences by absorbing some additional resources (mature students) during recessions as unemployment rises and by releasing some during periods of recovery. However, it is hard to detect these shifts even in such detailed measures of ''retention rates'' from the fifth grade up and into college entrance as are now available [25, p. 40].

The strong upward trend in the quantity of resources entering into education is also relevant in this connection; for example, in the United States, between 1900 and 1956, although the number of teachers rose only from 1.86 to 2.34 percent of the employed labor force, the number of mature students (in high school and in higher education) rose from 3.5 to 16.5 percent relative to the employed labor force [19, Table 2; also 1, Table 14]. Economic instability which results in large changes in the general level of prices bears heavily on education because the educational sector is inherently slow in adjusting to such changes in over-all prices. Much has been said about the adverse effects of inflation upon the quality (competence) of the individuals who are recruited and induced to stay in teaching. The extent of these adverse effects has not, however, been investigated.

Suppose we treat schools as if they were firms and the educational establishment as if it were an industry [139]. How efficient is schooling by normal standards of resource allocation? Surely the optimizing principles on which an important part of economic theory rests are applicable. There are, however, as yet few studies. Nor do I pursue this area of inquiry beyond mentioning it.

I am aware that in school circles the term "efficiency" carries adverse connotations – it implies the efficiency expert with no respect for the human factor in learning and with an over-emphasis on how classrooms are arranged, on the introduction of mechanical teaching devices, and on other changes in structures and equipment. "Efficiency" can be pursued, and undoubtedly it often is, with no reliable measures of the real and important differences in the quality of teachers. There is also the ever-present question: How can one gauge efficiency in schooling with no concepts of the quality of the "output" that can be identified and measured? These misgivings about the concept of efficiency applied to schooling are not groundless; moreover, applications of the optimizing concepts of economics to schools are beset with unresolved difficulties [14].

Without being a devotee of "efficiency," I have convincing reasons for believing that the allocation of resources within schools and between schools matters. It would be surprising if there were not some major "inefficiencies" in the way resources are used in education, given the history of its growth, the changes in relative factor prices that have occurred, and the weak incentives that exist in much of education to adjust to changes in the value of schooling and to changes in the prices of the resources employed, even if there were no technical developments whatsoever relevant to education. There is the traditional long summer vacation, which suited the requirements of an agrarian society but which is not well designed for a highly urbanized society. A strong case can be made that all too little has been done to economize on the time of students because the time of students is commonly treated as if it were costless. Yet, in fact, as I shall show later, the earnings that students forego while attending high school and college are more valuable than all of the other resources employed in education at these two levels. Then, too, the value (price) of human effort of both teachers and students has been rising markedly relative to the price of material inputs. Such a large shift in the relative price of inputs argues for the substitution of material inputs for human effort wherever this is feasible. But is it possible? The facts are far from clear.

There also is a strong presumption that those who make the "production" decisions for education do not give sufficient thought to the changes in the demand for their products. Following Stigler [134], a test can be made to determine whether enough is spent on the search for information. It would appear that both private and public decisions affecting the allocation of resources to education are based on unnecessarily vague information about prospective demands for the skills and knowledge that education produces. These decisions, moreover, are made in an institutional setting that blunts private initiative and swamps public policy with other considerations.

Lastly, there is Coombs' query [196]: How satisfactorily does the educational establishment perform in developing and adopting new techniques? By new techniques I mean new kinds of inputs that are superior to some of the inputs that are being employed in producing educational services. The notion of new and better techniques in this context includes additions to knowledge. Little indeed is known about the introduction of such new and superior resources within the educational establishment [19, pp. 82-84].

The costs and the value of schooling will be treated at some length in later sections. The other two issues - schooling and the business cycle and efficiency in the way in which schools are run - will not be pursued beyond this point. I have deliberately as yet not discussed the relations between policy and economic analysis, for in education, as in other areas, these relations require and deserve a section in their own right. I now turn to them.

Where Policy and Economics Join

The common school in the United States is predominantly a public school and is inescapably in the mainstream of public policy, and the major underlying policy questions are not altogether new. Despite all that has been said to the contrary, schooling has received a high rating over the decades. Horace Mann, a commanding figure in the early public school movement, saw universal education as the "great equalizer" of man's conditions, the "balance wheel of the social machinery," and the "creator of wealth undreamed of." The idea of universal education was at that time "a radical notion shared by a shaky alliance of farmers, workers, and businessmen" [111, p. 9]. A "free" common school did become a political reality.

Once the common school had been won, there began the almost continuous transformation of the school. The Grange, representing farm people, wanted some practical agricultural training. The rise of industry and the decline of apprenticeships created a demand for some vocational education. There were a few agricultural and industrial leaders who saw the benevolent influence of science and technology. Major cultural adjustments were also necessary because of the changing national community. It was a

major task to *Americanize* the many immigrants, and to *Civilize**
the newly developing industrial economy with its new forms of
poverty, slums, and unsettled neighborhoods. In addition, the
rural community needed assistance to check deterioration. Each
of these required adjustments, and education was always viewed
as a primary instrument. Each new social reform was soon linked
to particular educational reforms. Meanwhile, the idea of the
public school was extended to include the high school and the
state university. The land-grant colleges and universities are
already celebrating their first centennial. But policy questions
pertaining to education are far from settled, and the further
transformation of the school continues.

Where, then, do public policy pertaining to education and economic analysis join? I shall first examine a view which is based
on the belief that the right questions for economic research are
policy questions and that those who understand the policy issues
can formulate these questions. Next, I shall mention in passing
some of the school issues that appear to be of major public concern and then, based on recent research in this area, indicate
what its implications are for policy.

Pursuing a Mirage. Although there is much wisdom in the
phrase "the first move of importance in the game of research is
to ask the right question," it can be very misleading. It misleads
those who come to believe that in research the right question is
known or readily knowable, hence waiting to be asked; and that
a major fault of research people is that they proceed by muddling
rather than by first asking the right question. Accordingly, having come to this view, there is then much to be said for having
someone whose job it is to ask the right questions. What could
be simpler?

Who, then, is qualified to ask such questions? Obviously, it
cannot be the muddlers, for they are too close to the data and too

---

*See Professor John Nef's conception of "civilization" in *Civiliza-*
tion, Industrial Society and Love. Occasional Paper of the Center for
the Study of Democratic Institutions. Santa Barbara, California, 1961.

committed to a theory. It must be an intelligent person who believes in research and who specializes in asking these questions. This reasoning opens strange doors. Congressional committees come to believe that they are well qualified to tell research workers who are supported by federal funds what they should investigate; foundations are also inclined to select the major research questions, although with more regard than Congress for the views of those who think of themselves as "authorities" in a particular field; even universities lean increasingly toward organized research headed by research administrators who presumably either know the right questions or know how to proceed to discover them.[†] Despite all of these views and efforts, the right questions remain among the real unknowns in the game of winning new knowledge by means of research.

Scientists and others who do research are not without blame for these mistaken views about research. Those who have been successful in making a major contribution to knowledge correctly emphasize the importance of having formulated the right question, but some of them incorrectly leave the impression that they undertook the research with prior knowledge about the precise question to be investigated, and thus they fail to make explicit to others that the formulation of the question which proved to be the rewarding one was achieved as an integral part of the research process. Meanwhile, much is said and written on the need for basic research. But who can determine the studies that will prove to be *basic* research?[*] Surely it will not be done by members of a Congressional committee, or by the staff of foundations, or by private individuals who support research, or by university

[†]See my "Economic Policy Research for Agriculture," *Canadian Journal of Agricultural Economics,* IX, No. 2 (1961), 97–100.

[*]The National Science Foundation, in its annual survey of resources entering into research and development, distinguishes between basic and applied research on the basis of the motivation of those doing the research. Basic research is by definition that research "in which the primary aim of the investigator is a fuller knowledge or understanding of the subject under study, rather than ... a practical application thereof." In making these surveys there is a quibble about "general-pur-

research administrators. Nor do scientists and scholars really know in the sense of having correct prior knowledge of which questions will lead to basic results. What is in fact *basic* research is an ex post evaluation; basic research is research that did in fact make a fundamental contribution to knowledge. The lesson to be drawn from the work of those who have succeeded in doing basic research is that there is no royal road that leads to new knowledge. Moreover, it is presumptious to say, "these are the right questions"; the unknown inherent in any future research that will prove to be rewarding makes such a statement absurd.

Let me anticipate a criticism of the preceding remarks. Some may argue: "While these remarks may be accepted as applicable to the prestige sciences—physics, chemistry and biology—they may not be relevant to research in economics, because economics is different by virtue of the fact that it is a study of the social behavior of people." It will also be said that the contributions of economics are, above all, in the area of policy and that competent lay leaders who are concerned about policy have for this reason special qualifications for identifying important policy questions.

Questions pertaining to national policy have, of course, long been in the forefront in economics. A strong case could be made for the view that much of what we think of as economics had its origin in response to major unsettled policy questions that attracted competent minds with a talent for economic analysis. Three such questions come readily to mind. In England, the difficulties of growing enough food domestically as industrialization proceeded was a major factor, no doubt, in inducing Ricardo and other English economists of that period to clarify the underlying

---

pose" and "mission-oriented" research in the underlying definition. But this aside, the key to their definition is in what is presumed to be the motivation of the investigator. But until it has been established that these declarations of motives are indeed associated with research results, that is, in the one case they make basic contributions and in the other they do not, the motivational definition is an act of faith, at best a "working hypothesis."

costs conditions and the implications of freer trade. The mass unemployment of the thirties challenged, among others, Keynes; and his thinking about economic instability added a major dimension to economics. The large, continuing adjustments in resource allocation associated with economic growth in high-income countries, notably the adjustments required in agriculture under modern conditions are also attracting the attention of economists.

Unsettled policy questions as comprehensive as those referred to above were never nicely formulated and neatly packaged ready for research. They were at the time a jumble of ideas. Only later, in retrospect, are they euphemistically referred to as clear and cogent issues in the intellectual climate of the time.

No Paucity of Policy Issues. A mere mentioning of some of these issues will serve to show that the economic component need not loom large in some of them. Public discussions of school policy range from such basic constitutional questions as the separation of church and state and the integration of schools to such trivial issues as the readoption of the McGuffey Reader by a local school board. While economists can help clarify the underlying issues of the old, continuing debate about federal aid for education, these issues cannot be settled by economic analysis alone. The issues associated with contract research and research grants in providing public funds to universities are predominantly not economic in character, although funds for research compete for teaching talent.

The growth in population makes it necessary to increase the number of classrooms. Schools must adjust to the shifts in school-age population that are a consequence of the vast amount of internal migration. People want more and better schooling as revealed in the aspirations of parents and students in their demand first for universal elementary schooling, then for high school education, and now for higher education for a large and increasing proportion of young people. These developments raise some economic issues that matter. So do scholarships, whether supported by private or public funds, aid to depressed areas for schooling to retrain adult workers, the support of vocational schooling, and still others.

But the main public concern pertains to the continuing transformation of schooling and the educational establishment. As Cremin [111] in his brilliant historical study of the period between 1876 and 1957 shows, this has long been a major public purpose throughout the United States. Education and democracy have been closely linked in the trials and errors underlying the public effort to improve the schools.

From Economics to Policy. How much traffic is there on the road that runs from economics to policy? To return to some of the broad economic policy issues already discussed, the intellectual foundations for free trade policy were built by economists. So was the rationale for modern fiscal and monetary policy. Similarly, economists who are analyzing the investment attributes of education are laying the *foundations for an economic growth policy which assigns a major role to schooling and to the advance in knowledge that is won by those in the educational establishment.* In a concluding note on policy in "Investment in Human Capital," I [67] have elaborated in some detail on these and related issues.

II. COSTS OF EDUCATION

If education were free, people presumably would "consume" it until they were satiated, and they would "invest" in it until the return to education was zero. But attending school is far from free, as is well known. What is not known, however, is that schooling is much more costly than is shown in school expenditures because earnings foregone by mature students do not appear as an expenditure. In this section I examine the costs of schooling; usually it will be the costs of a year of schooling. I do not, however, consider separately each of the several costs incurred by the educational establishment, for if I did it would also be necessary to examine the costs of such activities as university research where they do not directly serve instructional purposes. My purpose is to ascertain the factor costs of schooling. There are a number of conceptual problems which arise mainly from the inclusion, as is necessary, of particular opportunity costs. The rewards, however, of working with an all-inclusive concept of costs in studying schooling are many. An array of issues about education that have baffled investigators will become clear. I also comment on the difficulties that arise when one attempts to determine who it is that bears the costs of education. Since most treatments of the costs of schooling are based on data drawn from statistics of "school expenditures," the relevance of these data will be discussed.

The concept of school expenditures, whether for public or for private schools, is not appropriate for the purpose of ascertaining all of the costs of education. Statistics of school expenditures are an odd collection of current operating expenses, capital outlays for land, structures, and equipment, and then a list of auxiliary items that have little to do with schooling. Moreover, regardless of how adequate the statistics, school expenditures do not include all of the costs incurred in schooling; nor do they cover all of the costs that are not borne by the student or his family. But expenses incurred by students, or their families, are equally inappropriate for this purpose, for obviously they do not include all of the costs of schooling; nor do they come even close to covering all of the costs that are borne by students or their families; for they omit the school taxes borne by them, the financial aid given by them in the case of parochial schools, and the opportunity costs that are represented by earnings that students forego while attending school.

For the purpose at hand, one wants a concept that will account to the economy for *all* the annual costs of schooling. One thus wants to identify and measure all of the input services entering into schooling; or, in other words, the real factor costs of schooling. I shall refer to this concept of costs as the "total factor costs" of schooling. In most industrialized nations *the larger part* of these costs beyond the elementary years is borne by the student or his family. Here one must include, in addition to tuition and other explicit outlays and the not so explicit earnings foregone, the taxes, mainly local school taxes, paid by the family where children attend a public school, or "gifts" by the family to finance a parochial school where children attend it, and the "profits foregone" in case they own stocks in corporations that make grants to the school which the children attend. *The smaller part* of these costs is borne by persons other than the student or his family through taxes and grants made directly to the school, or indirectly through corporations in which they have stocks, and through grants made to schools by private foundations.

As one comes to see clearly the magnitudes of each of these classes of costs, that is, costs borne by the student,[†] costs not borne by the student, and the sum of the two giving us the *total factor costs* of the schooling, one gains new perspectives with respect to the economics of education. It has already been noted

---

[†]Hereafter I shall frequently omit the phrase "by his parents" or more accurately "by his family." Thus it should be kept in mind that when I say "borne by the students," I mean to include the costs borne by the students' families.

that the costs borne by students are the larger part of total factor costs, although the common impression is to the contrary. I shall pursue this matter far enough a little later to leave no doubt that in the United States the costs borne by students is much the larger of the two. Nevertheless, to the extent that students do not bear all of the costs of their schooling and if such schooling has the attributes of an investment because it increases the future earnings of students, the rate of return to the costs they have borne will be higher than the rate of return to the total factor costs incurred. Students may earn on their outlay what is in fact an attractive rate compared to the rate of return to be had on alternative investment opportunities, while for the economy as a whole it may be an unattractive investment by the same criterion, that is, measured by the rate of return on alternative investments. It would be premature, however, to deduce from this relationship that students generally overinvest in education in the sense that the rate of return to total factor costs of school-ing are significantly below the general rate of return to other in-vestments. Although the "incentive to overinvest" is present, there are strong reasons for believing it may be swamped by other considerations. In the first place, when earnings foregone are reckoned, the proportion of total factor costs borne by stu-dents becomes as a rule so large that the differences between what students bear and total factor costs is relatively small. In the next place, there are these matters: Students are unsure of their talent for learning in school because they commonly dis-cover them only by going to school; students are investing in skills and knowledge which will serve them over four decades and longer, and the value of an asset with so long a life span is beset by many uncertainties; they are seldom well informed even when it comes to job opportunities in the near future, namely, about jobs and earnings likely to await them when they complete their schooling; and finally, even though students come to be-lieve that they have the necessary talents and that prospective earnings warrant their investing in more schooling, they will dis-cover that the capital market is still very imperfect in lending funds to students, and especially so if the funds that are being sought are to cover both tuition and earnings foregone.

Who bears the costs of education is indeed a basic matter in studying the allocation of resources to education and in examining the effects of alternative ways of financing education upon the personal distribution of income among families and upon their welfare. But at this point I must place this matter aside and return to the concept of *total factor costs* of education. Obviously if there were estimates of all of the costs borne by the student and of all the costs not borne by him, I could merely add these two components. Such estimates, however, are not at hand; moreover, they require much painstaking work. Fortunately, it is much easier to estimate total factor costs directly.

With this aim in mind, it will be convenient to distinguish between the costs of the educational services provided by schools and the opportunity costs of the time of students while attending school. Ideally, for the first of these, economists want a measure of the annual flow of the inputs employed for education. This flow consists of the services of teachers, librarians, and school administrators, of the annual factor costs of maintaining and operating the school plant, and of depreciation, obsolescences, and interest. It should not include expenditures to operate particular auxiliary enterprises, such as providing school lunches, room and board for students, and operating "organized" athletics or other noneducational activities. School expenditures for scholarships, fellowships, and other financial aids to students should also be excluded, because they are in the nature of transfer payments* [18]. For the second, estimates of the earnings that students forego while attending school are required.

But instead there exist mainly statistics covering public school expenditures and school budgets. Statistics for private schools are hard to come by, especially for elementary and secondary schooling. Capital outlays are frequently reported as if they were exhausted in the year they were made, and there is little to go on in estimating depreciation, obsolescence, and imputed interest on the durable facilities used for education. Then, too, school budgets include some expenditures that must be iden-

---

*If they were to be viewed as "earnings," then the estimate of earnings foregone should be reduced accordingly.

tified and excluded for the purpose at hand. As already noted, board and room for students should be put aside. (Economists do not add what a worker spends on food and housing to his wages when they estimate labor costs of an industry.)

The next step will be to examine briefly particular studies of costs of schooling to show what they contribute to our search. I begin with studies restricted to public school expenditures and then proceed to studies which include both public and private school expenditures. But before I consider total factor costs, I shall examine in some detail the important cost component which I have been referring to as "earnings foregone."

Public School Expenditures

School expenditures by public bodies are the most readily available statistics. They are, of course, used for purposes other than estimating the costs of education. To clarify the conceptual limitations of these statistics for the purpose at hand, I turn to three quite different studies.

1. A ninety-page statement by the Committee for Economic Development, *Paying for Better Public Schools,* shows that public school expenditures in the United States rose from $2.3 to $14.4 billion and from 2.4 to 3.1 percent of gross national product between 1929-30 and 1958-59 [110]. These estimates are restricted to *public* elementary and secondary schools, borrowed funds are included, and gross capital outlays† are attributed to the year in which they are incurred. (There is no attempt to estimate net as against gross investment in school buildings, etc., or to transform capital outlays into annual input services.) Estimates such as these are of little value in determining the annual factor costs of education, however useful they were in preparing this particular policy statement.

2. A study by Edding is noteworthy, although it too is based predominantly on public school expenditures [7]. Edding exam-

---

†The $3.6 billion given for capital outlays in 1958-59 is substantially in excess of the capital outlay reported in U. S. Department of Health, Education, and Welfare, *Health, Education and Welfare Trends,* 1961 edition, p. 54.

ines 24 countries in considerable detail, along with long series of historical data for a number of these countries. Only a few minor estimates are included which cover both public and private schools. Edding makes a number of international comparisons to show the relationship mainly between public school expenditures and national income. These comparisons, however, are subject to considerable error because of the fact that private school expenditures are not taken into account and because these vary substantially among countries. The omission of earnings foregone by students presents a more serious limitation in interpreting these international comparisons. For example, the estimates for the Soviet Union include stipends that substitute for a large component of what would be earnings foregone in the United States.

3. Martin and Lewis [15] in a useful study compare the revenue and public expenditures of 16 countries at different levels of economic development. Their purpose is to see how patterns of expenditure and sources of revenue vary with economic development. They introduce the concept of "basic" current expenditure in treating capital outlays and use it as an analytical tool. While it is not their purpose to estimate the total factor costs of education or of any of the other major activities which they examine, the limitations of these statistics in gauging the costs of education arise from the fact that neither private school expenditures nor earnings foregone by students is included.

Public Plus Private School Expenditures

Private school expenditures are not negligible. In 1956 the private educational sector provided about 12 percent of all elementary and secondary schooling and about 42 percent of the higher education in the United States, based on annual factor costs other than earnings foregone by students* [18, Tables 3 and 4].

*Measured by total current expenditures, capital outlay, and interest, the respective percentages were 15 and 41 in 1961. See U. S. Department of Health, Education, and Welfare, *Trends,* 1961 edition, p. 53.

Wiles' [80] treatment of the 1953 "intellectual investment" of Great Britain breaks new ground conceptually. He extends the concept of schooling to include off-campus courses ranging from studies that are offered in night schools and in "ten week seminars on current affairs." These and others he classifies as "further education" and proceeds to estimate the expenditures for this purpose. He then considers "apprenticeship schemes, management training, training within industry, borstals, vocational and disabled training, industrial rehabilitation, private tutorial and commercial colleges, correspondence courses and private tuition." The total costs which he reckons for these seem too small. He then takes the important step of introducing "the opportunity cost of keeping pupils of 15 and over away from production." This concept is an approach to "earnings foregone," to be considered below. Wiles uses "a fair maintenance charge" in estimating this item; this is not correct, because cost of living that enters into maintenance would exist whether these young people were holding jobs or attending school, except for a small difference to the extent that somewhat better clothes and some additional travel are required while attending school. Wiles' overall estimates for 1953 are as follows: gross *current* educational expenditures are 2.7 percent of gross national product,[†] and net educational expenditures, a measure of the net addition to the capital stock of education of Great Britain, comes to 1.25 percent of net national income. He gives no estimate of the capital stock of education.

Vaizey [26] in his *The Costs of Education* in the United Kingdom covers both public and private schooling and in a much needed historical perspective. Estimates for England and Wales,

---

[†]Martin and Lewis, cited above [15], Table II, give the "basic" current public expenditures for education in the United Kingdom for 1953-54 as 3.47 percent of gross national product. Conceptually, Wiles includes a number of cost components that are not in the estimates of Martin and Lewis. Vaizey [26], discussed below, in Table III places public and private educational expenditures in the United Kingdom at 3 percent of national income in 1955 (also about 3 percent is indicated for 1953). Wiles' estimates compared to these seem substantially too low.

Scotland, and Northern Ireland are presented separately. Thus it should be feasible to measure the effects of schooling upon the economic capabilities of the people of Scotland and of those of England and Wales, using Vaizey's estimates and historical materials. Such a study would seem to be overdue in view of the strong presumption that differences in amounts spent on education have been an important underlying economic factor in favor of Scotland. The treatment of costs by Vaizey is subject to two limitations: a minor one—capital outlays for public schools are not transformed into "current inputs," although in the case of private education, costs are based on fees and these presumably include rent on the land and school facilities which also cover depreciation and obsolescence; and a major omission—no estimates are included for the opportunity cost of the time of students, hence no account is taken of earnings foregone.

Opportunity Costs of the Time of Students

Students in secondary schools and beyond, and many of them before they have completed their elementary schooling, could be earning their keep and more at jobs suitable to their age and experience. Thus, there is here an *opportunity cost* in attending school that is equal to the earnings that students forego.

One of the puzzles about the literature in this field is that this important cost component of education has been so long neglected. Cultural history may explain this omission. Throughout most of western Europe, secondary schooling has served mainly to prepare a small, select group of students for higher education, and the functions of the university have been to instruct students for particular elite roles. Sir Eric Ashby [143] states this orientation of universities succinctly:

"From Bologna and Salerno comes the function of the university to train students for certain professions, like the church, medicine, and law. From Oxford and Cambridge comes the university's function as a nursery for gentlemen, statesmen and administrators. From Göttingen and Berlin comes the function of a university for scholarship and research."

Most of these university students came from families who did not expect their children to enter the rank and file of the labor force. They could afford leisure for themselves and roles for their children which would carry prestige and influence. These elite expectations along with a gentle sprinkling of scholarships served as cultural blinders making it difficult to see that students might be foregoing earnings while attending school. Modern cultural developments, which include advances in science and technology, have extended greatly the functions of education and have increased markedly the number and the proportion of young people attending school beyond the elementary level, notably in the United States and more recently in the Soviet Union. It is indeed meaningful, under these circumstances, to recognize the value of the time students spend in school and to reckon the earnings that students forego.

I have presented elsewhere[18] in some detail a logical basis for the concept of earnings foregone and a method by which they can be estimated. It will not be necessary therefore to burden this essay with these conceptual issues, except to consider, as will be done below, the need of scrutinizing with care both the concepts and the available estimates.

To acquire a sense of the magnitude of earnings foregone, it will be helpful to compare them with the other costs of schooling. Let me draw on estimates which I made some time ago for the United States. These estimates indicate that for 1956 the earnings foregone by high school students came to nearly $6.6 billion while the other costs entailed in this schooling were $4.3 billion, and that for college and university students the respective amounts were $5.8 billion and $4.1 billion. Accordingly, for both classes of students, earnings foregone accounted for about three-fifths of the total factor costs of their education.

Preliminary estimates by Carnoy [3, Tables 7 and 8] for Mexico are similar with respect to the relation between these two sets of costs. Total costs in 1957 for secondary schooling in Mexico came to 1.240 million pesos, of which 760 million were earnings foregone. It should be borne in mind, however, that secondary schooling in Mexico begins after the completion of only six years of primary schooling. Moreover, in a low income country like Mexico, there are earnings foregone for students who are very young, at age 12 and perhaps even at age 10. For university and polytechnic education in Mexico the 1957 estimates for total costs are 390 million, of which 220 million pesos consisted of earnings foregone.

It is in the annual costs of schooling per student that one can best see the role that earnings foregone play. In Table 1 estimates are shown for two high and two low income countries. The

Table 1. School Costs, Earnings Foregone, and Total Costs of Schooling per Student Per Year in the United States, Israel, Mexico, and Venezuela

	School Costs	Earnings Foregone	Total	Earnings Foregone as Percentage of Total Costs
United States, 1956 (dollars)				
8 years elementary	280	0	280	0
4 years high school	568	852	1,420	60
4 years college or university	1,353	1,947	3,300	59
Israel, 1957-58 (Israeli pounds)				
8 years primary	140	30	170	18
4 years post primary	670	1,000	1,670	60
3 years higher education	2,481	2,930	5,411	54
Mexico, 1957 (pesos)				
6 years primary	(360)	0	(360)	0
6 years secondary	1,794	2,833	4,627	61
3 years university	2,426	3,280	5,706	57
Venezuela, 1957-58 (bolivars)				
6 years primary	400	0	400	0
5 years secondary	1,200	5,000	6,200	81
4 years university	5,000	12,000	17,000	71

Source: United States [19, Table 6]; Israel [41, from data appearing on p. 149]; Mexico [3]; and Venezuela [73, Chapter XV]. Figure in parentheses for Mexico are mine based on very tentative data.

findings for Israel and the United States, shown in the last column, are remarkably similar. The differences between them are consistent with one's expectations, that is, in Israel, where incomes are substantially below those in the United States, there are some earnings foregone in the 8 years of primary schooling. The estimates for Mexico and Venezuela point up the fact that earnings foregone become large relative to total costs after only 6 years of schooling. My belief is that some earnings foregone start with the fourth and fifth year of schooling.

It has already been noted that there are a number of puzzles related to education for which earnings foregone offer a consistent and unified explanation. Let me comment on a number of these. (1) Mincer [60] shows that there has been a shift from training on-the-job to learning in schools. Since foregone earnings are larger relative to the total costs of on-the-job training than they are to the total cost of schooling, this difference may be a key to this shift. The costs of learning on-the-job when the training is not specific to the labor requirements of the firm is, presumably, all borne by the employee in lower wages, that is, through earnings foregone; whereas not all of the costs of learning in schools are borne by students. For students in the United States who are beyond the elementary grades, about three-fifths of the costs are also earnings foregone as indicated above, but of the rest at least a part is as a rule on public account or borne by private grants to schools. (2) The average daily school attendance of children from farm homes tends to be lower than that of children from nonfarm homes. There is much work on farms that children can do and many farm families are relatively poor, which makes the value of the work that children can do for them by missing a few days of school now and then rate comparatively high. (3) It has been widely observed that although tuition is free, or scholarships are provided to cover tuition and more, many talented children from low income homes do not avail themselves of the additional educational opportunities. The reasons usually given for their choice have been cultural and social. But one of the principal reasons is undoubtedly the importance of the earnings foregone in these circumstances. (4) Only a small proportion of the children in most low income countries complete the primary grades. The conventional costs of providing this schooling appear very small even for many low income countries. But if it is true that children at a tender age, say beginning at age 10, are required to work to piece out the meager family income, the value of this work by children may loom large in the minds of parents as a cost of such schooling. (5) Other issues in which the earnings that students forego are a major factor include the amount to be loaned to students, the modification of tax laws to treat schooling as an investment in human capital and the adjustment of the concept of national income referred to below. Estimates of the rate of return to investment in schooling would be all too high if foregone earnings were not included as a cost of schooling, and, more generally, the true costs of schooling to students and to the economy would be seriously underestimated if earnings foregone were not reckoned.

In view of the importance of earnings foregone as a component in the costs of schooling and the difficulties in getting at them, the logical basis of this concept and the techniques and data used in making estimates must be scrutinized with care. How people use their income is a matter of taste, and taste is not independent of cultural considerations. Much can be done, however, by abstracting from differences in taste and treating earnings foregone as if they were bound by economic restraints, predominantly by the income of people. Like leisure, earnings foregone are related to the level of income. The hypothesis would be that as income rises, the age at which children are expected to do productive work and thus earn also rises. People in low income countries, as has already been pointed out, expect children to enter upon useful, regular work, say, at age 10; as countries rise on the income scale, the age at which children are expected to take jobs also rises.

Would students who are attending high school or college earn more than those who are of the same age groups but who are not in school? Because of differences in ability, the answer would seem to be in the affirmative. Blitz [2] has investigated this issue and his findings show that these differences are substantial; thus, estimates of earnings foregone based on the earnings of

those youths who are not in school to this extent tend to understate the earnings foregone for those attending school. Are the
earnings of high school and college students negligible during
the school terms? There was no way of knowing until recently
when the Bureau of Labor Statistics in one of its surveys undertook to find out how many hours a week students were employed.
It turns out to be substantial. In the fall of 1959, 22.6 percent of
all the enrolled students in the United States aged 14-17 were
employed, working an average of 11.4 hours per week. Of those
who were 18-24 years of age, 39.8 percent were employed, working an average of 25.7 hours per week. Unless the earnings ob-
tained for this work are taken into account, estimates of earnings
foregone based on the assumption that students give all of their
time to their studies would to this extent overstate the earnings
foregone by students. Recent work by Griliches not yet published
shows that agricultural employment plays a larger part than might
have been expected in the work that young people do, and the effect of this is to reduce somewhat the earnings foregone by students compared to what they would be if this agricultural employment were not taken into account.*

Changes in the Costs of Education Over Time

The costs of schooling rise in a growing economy relative to
the size of the population and also relative to gross national
product, although little has been done to untangle this skein of
changing costs with a view to measuring and explaining them.
The two principal reasons underlying changes in costs arise out
of the increases in the amount of schooling produced and in the
supply price of the factors entering into it.

The amount of schooling rises more rapidly than the population because an increasing proportion attend school. But this
change has been for some decades a minor factor in the United
States since the total enrollment in all schools, public and pri-

---

*Zvi Griliches' study also suggests another agricultural effect, name-
ly, within agriculture the income foregone by children 10 to 13 years of
age while attending elementary school is substantial, actually about
one-third of that of high school students.

vate and from kindergarten to graduate instruction, only rose from 22.6 percent of the population in 1900 to 24.1 percent in 1930, and to 25.8 percent in 1960. The increase in number of days that enrolled pupils attend school has, however, played a large role; in public elementary and secondary schools this figure rose from 99 days per pupil enrolled in 1900, to 143 in 1930, and to nearly 160 days in 1960. Beyond the number of enrolled students and attendance, the amount of schooling rises for the simple reason that a year of secondary schooling and of higher education represents more schooling than a year of elementary schooling and that enrollment in the first two rises relative to the latter. Using costs of a year of schooling as the measure of the amount, a year of university work in the United States is nearly 12 times as large as that of a year of elementary schooling. Thus, the fact that the more expensive levels of schooling have been increasing at the higher rate becomes a major factor in the growth of schooling. For example, in the United States, whereas the total number of enrolled students rose 57 percent between 1930 and 1960, the enrollment in high school doubled, and undergraduates in higher education more than tripled. Those classified as graduate students rose almost eightfold, from 47,000 to 390,000.

Yet surely these increases in the "amount" of schooling are not the kind of trends that can be projected. The average daily attendance is reaching an upper limit. The proportion of young people embarking upon a high school education is also approaching a maximum, although the "drop out" rate could be reduced very substantially. On the other hand, the upper limit of the proportion of the college age group is not discernible as it is for elementary and secondary schooling [18, pp. 577-83].

The supply price of the factors entering into schooling rises with economic growth relative to consumer prices and also relative to the price of the factors entering into gross national product as is shown in Table 2. Let me comment on only one of these comparisons, that is, for the period between 1930 and 1956. During this period the consumer price index rose from 100 to 163, and the prices in gross national product to 189. The undeflated cost of a year of high school, however, rose to an index of over 364.

Table 2. Costs of Living and Gross National Product Prices
and Costs of Schooling per Enrolled Student in the
United States, 1900 to 1956

	Costs of Living 1947-49 = 100	Implicit Price Deflator Gross National Product 1954 = 100	Costs per Enrolled Student in Current Dollars		
			Elementary Adjusted for Attendance	High School	College and University
1900	36.0		23	115	378
1910	40.8		34	164	513
1920	85.7		60	375	995
1930	71.4	55.4	91	390	1,045
1940	59.9	48.9	90	409	1,087
1950	102.8	89.5	191	1,014	2,364
1956	116.2	104.6	278	1,421	3,305
Increase from 1900 to 1956 1900=100	323		1,209	1,225	874
Increase from 1930 to 1956 1930=100	163	189	305	364	316

Schooling is more dependent upon the human factor than is
production in the rest of the economy. In 1956 about 89 percent[†]
of the costs incurred for elementary and secondary schooling and
for higher education are attributed to labor. When earnings fore-

---

[†]Instruction and administration and, for higher education, also organized research, represented about 56 percent of all annual factor costs.
Add to this 75 percent of remainder, on the assumption that underlying
factor costs of the other inputs were like that of the economy as a
whole, and we obtain 56 + 33 = 89 percent. When earnings foregone are
included, about 73 percent of the direct annual factor costs are for
human effort plus 75 percent of the remainder, giving us 73 + 20 = 93
percent attributed to human effort.

gone by students are added, about 93 percent of the 1956 factor costs of education are traced back to wages and salaries for human effort.

Although one can make rough estimates, precise knowledge about the changes in the supply price of the inputs employed by schools is meager. Stigler [20] makes this abundantly clear in presenting teachers' salaries and in comparing changes in them with those of other "comparable" workers. Tickton [22], a decade later, provides a useful array of salaries for the period from 1904 to 1959. *Trends* [25] presents salaries of instructional personnel back to 1920. Even so, changes in the composition of teachers, their locations, their "quality," and changes in the supplemental incomes they receive and in conditions of employment leaves much to be desired when it comes to using these estimates.

The conclusion of this section points to a large increase in the quantity of schooling and to a marked rise in relative supply price of the factors entering into it associated with economic growth of the kind that has characterized the United States during recent decades. If it were true that the output per unit of input of the educational establishment remains essentially constant, there would be a strong presumption that the *real costs per unit of schooling rise markedly with economic growth.*

Some Unsettled Questions Regarding Costs

There are six questions related to scope, substantive issues about data, and to logic.

1. The scope of schooling can be defined variously depending upon the purpose of a study. The inquiry by Wiles [80] treats schooling broadly, going beyond that which is undertaken in elementary and secondary schools and in institutions of higher education. In his essay, "The Nation's Educational Outlay," Blitz [2] adopts a somewhat broader concept of schooling than I did [18]. Mine is restricted to elementary, high school, college and university education; his concept includes these and, also, commercial vocational schools, special residential schools, medical interns and residents, the educational component in special defense

programs, and other federal educational activities. These four items in 1955-56, according to Blitz [2, Table 2], cost $1.56 billion.

2. Schools generally receive special tax treatment; for example, they do not pay property taxes on school buildings, equipment, and facilities. Schools also as a rule are not required to pay sales taxes. Are these tax exemptions a real cost of schooling? Blitz includes the "imputed value of property and sales tax exemptions" which are granted to schools as costs and attributed $1.2 billion to these in his estimates for 1955-56. The logical basis, however, for including all of these tax exemptions as costs may be questioned [78, Appendix].

3. Thus, clearly since Blitz adopts a broader concept of schooling than I did and as a consequence includes $1.56 billion of additional school costs, and adds $1.2 billion for tax exemptions, his estimates of the total factor costs of schooling is to this extent larger than my estimate of $28.7 billion for 1956. But his estimate of total factor costs of schooling for 1955-56 is much larger still, for it comes to $37.1 billion. The principal source for this difference arises out of the fact that Blitz attributes $18 billion to earnings foregone, which is much larger than my estimate of $12.4 billion. The large upward adjustment that Blitz has made appears unwarranted for reasons that have already been covered. To repeat these reasons briefly, among the several factors which could affect my estimate, he examines those that would have the effect of increasing the estimate of earnings foregone but has not taken into account the offsetting factors which have the effect of decreasing this estimate.

4. There are among the cost components of schooling several items that logically belong in gross national product although they are not included presently. Moreover, the magnitude of these particular items that are omitted is large, and it would increase the gross national product appreciably if these items were included at factor costs.

5. At the outset of this chapter, I mentioned the importance of knowing who ultimately bears each of the several costs of schooling. There are some conceptual problems which require clarification. The main difficulties, however, arise in identifying

and measuring these costs for this purpose. Although the payment is indirect, it is nevertheless true that a student or his family may pay for much of the schooling he acquires through "gifts" in the case of parochial schools or through (local) taxes in the case of public schools.

6. The allocation of the costs of schooling between "consumption" and "investment in earnings" remains unsettled. Such allocations as have been attempted are inherently arbitrary because the logical basis for such allocations have not been formulated in ways so that estimates can be made. In practice, thus far, in estimating the rate of return to schooling from earnings, all of the costs of schooling are treated as if they were an "investment in such earnings," and none are allocated to "consumption," although it is obvious that for much schooling such a unilateral allocation is unwarranted.

III. ECONOMIC VALUE OF
EDUCATION

For purposes of economic analysis, a distinction is drawn between the consumer and the producer values of schooling, as I did in the introductory chapter. The contributions of schooling to consumption are then divided into those that serve consumption in the present and those that contribute to future consumption, and the latter become an investment. The producer values of schooling are straightway an investment in future capabilities to produce and earn income. Thus, in classifying the benefits of schooling, there are three conceptual boxes: (1) present consumption, (2) future consumption (an investment), and (3) future producer capability (also an investment). How large is each? No one really knows. There are studies that begin to show that the third box may be very large. Meanwhile, there are many signs that the other two may not prove to be empty, but what these signs really mean is as yet not known. As one gives thought to the taste, level of income, and costs of education in the United States, it would seem that only a small box is required for consumption in the present, while two large ones are needed for the other two classes of contributions of schooling, both of which are investments.

If all of the fruits of schooling entered directly into final consumption, additional schooling would not contribute to economic growth. More schooling would show up only in what people consumed as they responded to changes, including the rise in their income associated with economic growth. If, however, all of it took the form of enduring consumer capacities, additional schooling would enhance future well-being, but it would not appear in *measured* economic growth. Although real income would increase in terms of consumer satisfactions, the additional satisfactions from the investment in these enduring consumer capacities are not included in measured national income. Only if schooling increases future productivity and earnings do the contributions of schooling become *a source of measured economic growth.*

Again, it will be necessary to refer to the distinction between schooling and the educational establishment, because the schools which make up the educational establishment engage in a number of activities, the value of which does not enter into schooling, and because the value of schooling to the student depends in no small part on the efforts of the student to learn. It is all too easy to become bound to "teaching" and "learning" or to levels of schooling and classes of schools and miss some important functions of education. I propose, therefore, at this point to comment briefly on some of these functions.

Major Functions of The Educational Establishment

1. Research is one of the traditional functions of the educational establishment. The National Science Foundation [138] reports that in 1961 the professional staff of colleges and universities engaged in "basic" research in science was 45,000 full-time equivalent, with an assisting staff of 35,000 full-time equivalent. The total costs of this research in 1961, including salaries, overhead, equipment, facilities, and information, came to $0.9 billion. According to the NSF, half of all of the "basic" research in the United States was being done within colleges and universities. (Of the rest, a fourth was credited to other nonprofit institutions and the federal government and the other fourth to industry.) What is the value of this particular activity of colleges and universities? Although the NSF has developed a useful series of annual estimates of the costs of this research, it has not as yet succeeded in estimating the economic value of the research results. A classic study by Griliches* shows that the investment in hybrid corn research was yielding the U.S. economy, as of 1955, a return of about 700 percent per year. An estimate of the payoff to agricultural research as a whole suggests a rate

---

*Zvi Griliches, "Research Costs and Social Returns: Hybrid Corn and Related Innovations," *Journal of Political Economy,* 66 (October, 1958), 419-31.

of return of at least 35 percent a year. Denison [90, Table 32]
attributes about 18 percent (net) of the growth rate of the U.S.
economy between 1929 and 1957 to advance in knowledge.[†] But
what about that part of the advance in knowledge which originates from the research that is done in the colleges and universities? As yet, no one knows.

2. The educational establishment discovers and cultivates
potential talent. The capabilities of children and of mature students can never be known until they have been found and cultivated. Eckaus [91] presents the basis of this proposition succinctly: "It just does not seem to be true that human talent will
always appear no matter how discouraging the environment and
inadequate the cultivation. One of the functions of the educational system is to act as a mechanism for searching out and se-
lecting potential talent." The analogy with expenditures for exploration is close indeed. It is well known that it pays to invest
in oil exploration and in the improvement of extraction techniques. Similarly, it "pays" to have an educational system that
is organized to discover human talent and that seeks to improve
its techniques for achieving this objective. Reisman [216] sees
this function of education in depth and, also, how subtle the
process is.

3. Schooling increases the capability of people to adjust to
changes in job opportunities associated with economic growth.
When an established worker faces such adjustment, he may have
to leave his present occupation and enter upon another, and he
may also have to migrate out of a declining sector to one with
better job opportunities. The large movement of people out of
agriculture, made necessary because of the rapid rise in the productivity of labor in farming and because of the slow increase in
the demand for farm products, dramatizes the importance of these
adjustments. Under widely different circumstances, it is true that
individuals with 8 years of elementary schooling are better prepared to move and enter upon new jobs than are those who have
had only 4 or less years of schooling. Likewise, those with a

----

[†]When adjusted for sources which had negative effects, it is slightly
over 18 percent.

high school education are much better prepared to make such adjustments than are those who have completed no more than the elementary grades. Economic growth, under modern conditions, brings about vast changes in job opportunities.* Schooling in this connection is valuable because it is a source of flexibility in making these occupational and spatial adjustments.

4. Schools also recruit and instruct students for teaching, a traditional function of education. Even if *all* schooling were only for final consumption, teachers obviously would be required, that is, individuals with specialized learning – philosophers, scientists, and scholars for academic instruction and teachers for secondary and elementary schools. An investment would have to be made in this class of human resources in order to have the consumption already referred to. In 1956 teachers represented 2.3 percent of the employed labor force in the United States [19, Table 2]. Also relevant in the number that prepare for teaching is the fact that many elementary and high school teachers leave teaching after working at it for only a few years; the dropout rate of teachers is very high. The instructional staff for public schools may be 1.8 million by 1969, a rise of 26 percent during the decade of the sixties [25, p. 48], and the number of professional scientists and engineers who teach is projected to 175,000 by 1970, representing an increase of 75 percent above that of 1961 [138, p. 24]. Although one can readily identify these individuals and count them, the numbers by themselves do not tell what the skills and knowledge of this class of human resources are worth. Inside academies, there are mercenaries who entertain the thought that the pay is too low!

5. A commission report for Nigeria, *Investment in Education* [28], takes the stance that it is a part of the duty of an educational system of a country to meet the prospective needs for people with high skills and knowledge. The report proceeds to build on estimates of the future demand for high level skills of the rapidly growing economy of Nigeria and on the recommenda-

---

*In view of the divergency between private and social costs and returns in such situations, I have proposed "A Policy to Redistribute Losses from Economic Progress," *Journal of Farm Economics,* 43 (August, 1961). Also appeared in [131].

tions of Frederick Harbison [51; also see 157, 164]. Harbison stresses the key role of "high level manpower" in economic development, especially in low income countries. He uses a technique for estimating these prospective demands based on a combination of observable trends and simple projections. Such estimates of future high level manpower required can then be treated as goals for the educational system.

It is indeed one of the functions of education to serve a country in these respects. Much can be said for the Harbison approach where large changes and a rapid expansion in schooling is necessary to provide the skilled labor which a growing economy will soon need. An approach based on investment in schooling and on prospective returns, while more in line with the logical requirements for determining an optimum allocation and rate of return to investment, is much less direct and perhaps more difficult to apply under circumstances that characterize new nations launching programs to hasten their economic growth.

Education as a Source of Economic Growth

"Economic growth" has come to mean increases in national product, measured in constant "dollars." The study of this growth is presently high on the agenda of economists, not because of any commitment, naive or otherwise, to growthmanship but because of an increasing public concern about growth. But it has not been possible to explain the observed growth by the observed increases in conventional factors of production. The best clues are the improvements in the *quality* of factors, both man and machines, and in economies of scale. The amount of schooling, which has been rising rapidly, is being analyzed to see what effect it is having on the productivity of human effort. The contributions of university research to science and technology are also being examined to discover the extent to which they are a source of economic growth.

Arithmetic of Schooling and Growth. To clarify some general relations between schooling and economic growth, let me assume for sake of convenience that all schooling is an investment in earnings, that the rate of return is the same to each level whether it is elementary or a higher level of schooling, and that the

number of workers remains constant. Under these simplifying
assumptions, if the capital stock of schooling per worker were
not to rise, schooling would not be a source of economic growth.

Once a country attains a high level of schooling, although it
would undoubtedly require much schooling to maintain it and the
annual investment in schooling would be large, schooling would
obviously no longer be a source of economic growth. Also, however low the level, unless it is raised, schooling is not a source
of growth. Yet, starting from a low level, there are large possibilities for raising it. If the level were raised substantially and
rapidly, then during such a period schooling would be a substantial source of growth. Also, under these assumptions, adding
a year of high school per worker increases the capital stock of
schooling in the labor force much more than adding a year of elementary schooling. In the United States presently, as an investment, a year of high school costs about five times as much as a
year of elementary schooling. All of these relationships are
based on what happens to the capital stock of schooling per
worker. Once the assumption with respect to the constancy of
the size of the labor force is relaxed, then, even if per worker
schooling were to remain unchanged, any increase in the labor
force would increase the total capital stock of schooling and to
this extent it would become a source of economic growth.

To illustrate the arithmetic of growth, take an economy with
a 3 percent growth rate. Let the share of the national income
earned by labor be 75 percent and let additional schooling during
a year increase the productivity and earnings of labor by 1 percent. Schooling would then add 0.75 of a percentage point to the
growth rate, which would represent one fourth of the total growth
rate of 3 percent. (There also would be the additional schooling
represented by any increase in the labor force that occurs.) As
to the investment aspects, let the real earnings per worker be
$4,500 and the costs of the investment in the additional school-
ing which increases productivity and earnings by 1 percent be
$450. The implicit gross rate of return, disregarding depreciation
and obsolescence, is then 10 percent, simply because a 1 percent increase in earnings on $4,500 is $45 and thus a 10 percent
rate of return on the $450 invested.

Estimates and Implications. Two lessons may be drawn from studies that have been made of schooling as a source of economic growth. During the last three decades, schooling has been a larger source of growth than material capital represented by structures, equipment, and inventories as presently measured. The other lesson pertains to earlier decades and to the decades ahead. Between 1909 and 1929, as will be shown below, schooling played a much smaller role in growth than it has since then. During the next two decades the prospects are that schooling will continue to be a major source of growth, but beyond that it will not be possible to keep on increasing the capital stock of schooling at the rate which has characterized recent decades.

The rapid rise in schooling of members of the labor force in the United States accounts for about a fifth of the measured growth between 1929 and 1957. Years of school completed per person in the labor force rose from 8.41 in 1930 to 10.96 in 1957, which is an annual rate of 1 percent. Days of school attendance per year also increased rapidly. Adjusting for changes in average number of days of school attendance, counting a school year as 152 days, based on 1940, the equivalent school years completed rose from 6.01 to 10.45 between 1930 and 1957, which is an annual rate of slightly more than 2 percent [19, Table 7]. For the period between 1930 and 1960, Denison shows an increase of 34 percent in average number of years of school completed and also 34 percent for the average number of days of school attended per year of school completed. The product of these two developments gave an increase of 79 percent in the average total number of days of school attended, which is also an annual rate of increase of slightly more than 2 percent [90, Table 9].

A major, explicit assumption underlying the procedure used by Denison is the allocation of three fifths of the reported differences in earnings that correspond to differences in schooling to education. The other two fifths, it is assumed, is a consequence of associated characteristics [90, Table 8]. Suffice it to say that his procedure allocates about 21 percent of the economic growth of the United States between 1929 and 1957 to education.[†] The historical comparisons presented by Denison [90,

[†]In Table 32 on the sources of the growth in real national product, he allocates 23 percent of the growth rate between 1929 and 1957 to edu-

Table 32] lend support to the following inferences with regard to schooling: (1) The contribution of schooling to growth between 1909 and 1929 was a little more than one half of that between 1929 and 1957. (2) The projected 1960-80 growth from this source is a little less than that between 1929 and 1957. (3) For the longer run, it is impossible to maintain the *rate of increase* in the amount of schooling achieved during recent decades. (4) Between 1909 and 1929, material capital contributed to growth almost twice that of schooling, but between 1929 and 1957, the contribution of schooling exceeded that of material capital.

My estimate [19] of some time back for the period between 1929 and 1957, supports Denison. The approach that I used rests on estimates of the investment in schooling in people who are in the labor force and the rate of return earned on this investment. The first, expressed as a stock of capital in 1956 dollars, came to $180 billion for 1930 and to $535 billion for 1957. (A simple adjustment for trend indicates a stock of $173 billion for 1929.) Thus, the increase in this stock of capital between 1929 and 1957 comes to $362 billion. It should be noted that this approach allocates none of the costs of schooling in the labor force either to present or future consumption. These costs are treated as if all were solely an investment in future earnings. Three estimates of the rate of return were attempted. The two lower rates come to 9 and 11 percent [19, Table 18]. Applying these two rates to the increase in the capital stock of schooling of $362 billion, I obtain slightly less than $33 billion and $40 billion respectively as the growth in national income from schooling. If the national product increased $200 billion,* this additional schooling in the labor force accounts for 16.5, or 20 percent of

---

cation. This is a gross figure. Since there are among his "sources" some that have had a negative effect, his positive percentage points total 109, and the 23 percentage points attributed to education represent, therefore, about 21 percent of the positive sources of economic growth.

*In the essay "Education and Economic Growth, ' [19], the net national product estimates which I used rose from $150 billion to $302 billion in 1956 prices based on Kuznets' estimates. The. adjustment implied by going to Department of Commerce estimates appears to indicate a growth in national income of about $200 billion.

the total growth depending upon whether the 9 or 11 percent rate of return is employed.

Growth from Research. Measured by annual expenditures, half of the basic research in the United States is within the educational establishment [138]. How much does this research contribute to growth? Suppose one were to treat it as an investment. What is the rate of return? The advance in useful knowledge relevant to agricultural production has been large during recent decades. The return to agricultural research, mainly research within the land-grant colleges and universities and the U. S. Department of Agriculture, has been high.[†] For all basic research underway in colleges and universities, there are no useful estimates of return. At a much more general level, Denison [90] attributed somewhat more than 18 percent of the growth between 1929 and 1957 to advance in knowledge. To obtain this estimate, he allocated to this source the residual that he had left after accounting for all of the other sources which he had identified and measured. Obviously, his "advance in knowledge" includes several sources in addition to basic research. Nevertheless, the intuitive belief, widely held, that basic research is the mainspring to much useful knowledge and that the rate of return on it is high is presently the best basis for decisions, until ways are found of estimating these contributions.

Capital Formation by Education

From the evidence already presented, the picture is that schooling and advance in knowledge are both major sources of economic growth. It is obvious that they are not natural resources; they are essentially man-made, which means that they entail savings and investment. Investment in schooling is presently, in the United States, a major source of human capital.

Why insist on the concept of human capital? Is it not enough to analyze the amounts invested, the (marginal) rate of return, and the marginal effects of this class of investment upon the

---

[†]See President's Science Advisory Committee, *Science and Agriculture,* Agricultural Panel, January 29, 1962, Executive Office Building, Washington, D. C. (mimeographed).

growth in real national income? For many purposes these analytical steps would suffice. There are, however, some questions
about the behavior of an economy where the concept of human
capital is essential in winning answers. To clarify these, it will
be necessary to elaborate on how the omission of human capital
is very misleading. To do this, I shall have to repeat the essential argument that I have presented elsewhere [102].

A concept of capital restricted to structures, producer equipment, and inventories is all too narrow for studying either economic growth that is measured (national income), or, what is
more important, all gains in well-being from economic progress
(which also include the satisfactions that people derive from
more leisure, from the growing stock of consumer durables, and
from the satisfactions that come to people from better health and
more education – all of which are omitted in our present estimates of national income.) Kuznets sees the matter clearly at
one point in his most recent monumental study when he observes
that for "the study of economic growth over long periods and
among widely different societies – the concept of capital and
capital formation should be broadened to include investment in
health, education, and training of the population itself, that is,
investment in human beings. From this point of view the concept
of capital formation followed here is too narrow."* Only the
most diligent reader, however, will see and keep this limitation
in mind in drawing inferences from Kuznets' estimates and findings. It is the slowing down in the pace at which the particular
forms of material capital are formed that will be seen. But this
fact will not be related to the quickening pace in the formation
of human capital, nor to the even tempo of capital as an aggre-
gate.

Thus, a concept of capital that is restricted to structures,
producer equipment, and inventories may unwittingly direct attention to issues that are not central or critical in understanding
economic growth over long periods. The concern about the dis-

---

*Simon Kuznets, assisted by Elizabeth Jenks, *Capital in the Ameri-
can Economy: Its Formation and Financing*, p. 390. (A study by the
National Bureau of Economic Research.) Princeton: Princeton University Press, 1961.

tinct downward trend in the ratio of this type of investment (net material "capital" formation) to national income is one of these issues. Another is the importance that is attributed to the decline in the ratio of this class of capital to national income. There are no compelling reasons why the stock of any particular class of capital should not fall (or rise) relative to national income over time. Producer goods – structures, equipment, and inventories – are such a class. The fact, however, that investment in this class has been declining relative to the investment in human capabilities acquired by learning on-the-job and in schools and in other ways does raise major economic questions: Why has this shift occurred? Have the decisions which account for this shift been motivated by differences in return? Suppose, however, it were observed, which has not been the case, that the ratio of *all* capital to income had declined or had risen substantially. This might raise a fundamental issue pertaining to motives and preferences for acquiring and holding capital.

There is still another reason for insisting on the concept of capital in the case of schooling. Although the notion of "a year of schooling" is useful for some limited aims in studying education, years of schooling are not in general additive. The summation of years of elementary schooling and years of higher education is like adding things as unlike as rabbits and horses. Educational capital in a population or labor force, estimated simply at replacement costs even without any allowance for depreciation and obsolescence during the life of a people or during the years they are employed, is a far better measure of the amount of schooling than is a count of the number of years of school completed. In principle, the same reasons apply to subgroups, for example, engineers, chemists, physicians, and so on, although in practice the improvement in measurements is less because as a rule a subgroup is more homogeneous.

The connections between additions to a stock of capital as a store of wealth and the corresponding additions to output capacity are exceedingly intricate [31 and 48]. Things that differ only with respect to durability can differ in value as wealth although their annual output capacity at a given date is the same. The concept of a stock based on replacement costs is useful for some purposes despite its apparent simplicity. In the case of schooling, there is much to be said for the "Wonderful One-Hoss Shay" conception of depreciation which assumes that there is no depreciation (less plausible however for obsolescence) in the schooling that people have acquired from the time they enter the labor force until they retire. Needless to say there are alternative concepts and there is vast literature on this subject. Bowman [31] examines critically a number of variants and related concepts in relation to schooling.

A pervasive image of progress can readily blind the investigator to the fact that the educational capital in a country can also decline. Such a decline undoubtedly occurred during the recent past in East Germany as a consequence of the large outmigration of skilled technicians and of other persons with much schooling. Israel is a unique case in this respect, for here the pattern of in-migration for a time added many people with a high level of schooling to the population, which was followed by people entering who had much less schooling than the average of the then existing population. The Grunfeld and Ben-Porath study [41, pp. 146-50] of the per capita capital stock of schooling in Israel shows that there is evidence of a decline beginning in 1951, "which is explained by the inflow of immigrants mainly from Asia and Africa." This decline continued for several years at a moderate rate, leveling off toward the end of the decade. The total capital stock of schooling, nevertheless, increased during this period at an annual rate of about 2.6 percent because the growth in population more than offset the adverse effects of the observed decline in per capita schooling.

The educational capital in the labor force in the United States has been rising rapidly, increasing during recent decades at twice the annual rate at which "reproducible tangible wealth" has increased [102, p. 6]. The estimates that follow are based on 1956 price tags of a year of schooling [71]:

Elementary	$ 280
High school	1,420
College	3,300

The educational capital per member of the labor force rose from $2,236 to $7,555 in 1956 dollars between 1900 and 1957. It doubled between 1930 and 1957 (see Table 3). The total for all schooling in the labor force, of course, rose much more rapidly. It increased from $63 billion to $535 billion, in 1956 dollars, between 1900 and 1957 [71, Table 5].

As is shown in Table 4, Goldsmith's estimates of reproducible tangible wealth show an annual rate of growth of 2 percent between 1929 and 1957, whereas the growth rate of the educational capital in the labor force was a strong 4 percent [102, p. 6].

Investment in Education

Will This Debase Education? Once again it will be necessary to consider a preliminary matter before turning to the main purpose of this section, which is to treat a part of schooling and other functions of schools, for example, the research of colleges and universities, as an investment. But will this treatment not inevitably debase education? Surely it need not do so. The consumption benefits from schooling are not any the less valuable

Table 3. Capital Stock of Schooling per Person in the
U. S. Labor Force, 1900-1957

	Equivalent 1940 Years of Schooling Completed (per person)	Costs of an Equivalent Year of Schooling (in 1956 dollars)	Capital Stock of Schooling per Person in Labor Force (in 1956 dollars)
	(1)	(2)	(3)
1900	4.14	540	2,236
1910	4.65	563	2,618
1920	5.25	586	3,077
1930	6.01	614	3,690
1940	7.24	650	4,706
1950	8.65	690	5,969
1957	10.45	723	7,555

Source: Based on estimates appearing in [9] and [71].

Table 4. Estimates of Various Stock of Capital and Annual
Rates of Increase Between 1929 and 1957 in the
United States in 1956 Dollars

	1929	1957 (billion dollars)	Annual Rate of Growth (percent)	Rate Applied to 1957 (2) × (3) (billion dollars)
	(1)	(2)	(3)	(4)
1. Reproducible tangible wealth	727	1270	2.01	25.5
2. Educational capital in population	317	848	3.57	30.3
3. Educational capital in labor force	173	535	4.09	21.9

Sources: [102, Table 1].

Line 1: from Raymond W. Goldsmith, Statistical Appendix to *The National Wealth of the United States in the Postwar Period,* Table A-2, adjusted to 1956 dollars. Quoted with permission of Goldsmith.

Lines 2 and 3: from my essay "Education and Economic Growth," in N. B. Henry, Ed., *Social Forces Influencing American Education.* Chicago: University of Chicago Press, 1961, Table 14. With 1930 estimates reduced by 3.57 and 4.1 percent respectively to give estimates for 1929.

merely because it becomes known that there are also other benefits from schooling which increase future production and earnings.[†] On the contrary, the value of schooling will be enhanced
by more precise knowledge of its contribution to skills and other
capabilities which increase the earnings of human agents. Since

---

[†] As argued earlier in this essay, most of the consumption component
of schooling also has the attributes of an investment because of its
enduring quality and because of its favorable effects upon the future
satisfactions that people enjoy. Moral values, refinement of taste,
standards of conduct, and the art of living are all integral parts of this
consumption.

the concept of "investment" denotes something intrinsically "good," there is the ever-present temptation to exploit this concept by using it to promote expenditures that are not an investment, or that are a poor investment relative to other alternatives. No doubt there are those who will misuse such knowledge, yet this is not a valid reason for not pursuing it [69, 72]. The possibility of debasing education also arises in research, for here too since knowledge is sought by many scholars and scientists for its own sake, to safeguard this intellectual endeavor is a matter of concern. But the same reasoning which is applicable to schooling is relevant in the case of research.

It may be true generally that seeking knowledge for its own sake is really the best "policy" to advance basic research, even though the goal were theories and techniques that turn out to be useful in subsequent economic activities.

Effects upon Wage Structure and Income Distribution. The idea that some part of schooling is an investment has won support from three sets of studies. One of these, already considered in some detail, is in connection with economic growth. Another is in relation to the puzzle underlying the changes that have been occurring in the structure of wages and salaries. The third pertains to the decline in the inequality in distribution of personal income, which cannot be explained by the relatively small changes that have taken place reducing the concentration of the ownership of private wealth and increasing transfer payments. In each of these — growth, wage structure, and income distribution — changes in the amount of schooling becomes an important explanatory variable.

With respect to growth in the United States, there is now a considerable body of evidence which indicates that schooling and university research are major sources of growth. Let me add only two findings to those already presented. Harberger [50], observing the use of resources in Chile, attributes relatively large returns to schooling and to advance in knowledge. The Horvat [53] formulation of the optimum rate of investment for "underdeveloped" countries treats knowledge and skill as a critical investment variable in determining the rate of economic growth. *Knowledge* in his model is "the most important scarce factor."

Friedman and Kuznets [42], examining the income from independent professional practices, observe, among other findings, the effects of professional associations and governmental bodies in hindering entry, for example, into medicine and thus keeping the investment in these capabilities substantially below its optimum. The marked correspondence between education and earnings as an explanatory variable of the large income differentials between white and nonwhite workers in the United States is a major finding of Zeman [85]. The decline in the wages of skilled workers relative to unskilled workers [56, 106] misled earlier investigators into thinking that the rate of return to schooling and to on-the-job training is falling. The return to whatever is invested in such skills depends on the *absolute* differences in wages associated with the investment in skills and not on the relative wages. Over the long run, differences in the amounts invested in human capital in workers may be the single most important factor accounting for differences in wages.

Mincer [59] relates investment in human capital, consisting mainly of schooling, and the personal distribution of income. There is an awareness of this effect that goes back to earlier economic thought, for example, Dalton [35], but these treatments lack empirical content. The large differentials in earnings that correspond to differences in schooling have not gone unnoticed. Clark [34] has long stressed the investment side of schooling and the apparent large return. Glick and Miller [45] and Miller [58] relate the educational level of workers to their income. Houthakker [54], using the data from the 1950 census of population, related education and income on which Denison [89, 90] presumably has drawn. The review by Rivlin [217] of research in the economics of higher education is most useful in this connection.

A Part of Human Capital. Meanwhile, a general conception of investment in human capital has been formulated which includes not only a part of schooling but, also, parts of the expenditures on health, on-the-job training, the search for information about jobs, and on migration [70, 67]. An exploratory conference sponsored by the National Bureau of Economic Research — Universities Committee on Investment in Human Beings led to the prep-

aration of a number of important papers published as a supplement to the *Journal of Political Economy,* October, 1962. The
contribution by Becker [29] to this set is of major significance.

Becker started his study with the aim of estimating the return to college and high school education in the United States.
He soon discovered, however, as I note elsewhere [102], that
the investment activities related to schooling were akin to other
investment in people, and that all of these human investments
have a number of attributes in common for which received theory,
tailored to investments in structures and equipment, required reformulation. Becker derives the "exact and general relations between earnings, rates of return and the amount invested" and
shows "how the latter two can be indirectly inferred from earnings." He builds on these relationships by introducing particular
key attributes, that is, the costs of schooling, of on-the-job
training, and of other investments in man and the earnings pro-
files of workers of different ages. Becker then demonstrates that
this formulation of the underlying theory related to human investment offers a unified explanation of a wide range of empirical
phenomena.

Relating Costs to Benefits

Two Unresolved Problems. In matching the costs of schooling to each of the several benefits from schooling, assume that
the costs of schooling and that the person who bears these costs
are known. How is one to distinguish between consumption and
investment in future production capabilities in order to allocate
these costs? How is one to distinguish between those benefits
of schooling which accrue to the student and those which are
captured by other individuals (families)? Shaffer [72], Villard
[76], and Weisbrod [78] consider both the logical and empirical
sides of these problems. Shaffer is of the view that the empirical
task is essentially insurmountable. Villard and Weisbrod see the
logical pitfalls and seek an empirical course which will avoid
them.

In responding to Shaffer's comment, I [69] note that to follow
the easy procedure of treating all such costs as serving only
consumption will not do, but concur in the view that to allocate

all of them to investment in future earnings is fully as extreme
and unwarranted. Although the economic logic for allocating the
costs of schooling is clear and compelling, no one has as yet
developed a satisfactory empirical procedure for identifying and
measuring what in fact actually happens. With this difficulty,
any allocation, based on such clues as seem relevant, must in
all honesty be labeled "arbitrary." There is little intellectual
comfort in the knowledge that a similar brand of arbitrariness
characterizes other areas of analysis, for example, in the way
expenditures for electricity and for automobiles used by farmers
are divided and distributed between household and farm expenses.

In discussing the central question of allocating resources between consumption and investment in future earnings, Shaffer
emphasizes two facts, namely, that most students attend public
schools, and that up to a certain age school attendance is compulsory. But neither of these facts is relevant to a logical basis
for distinguishing between consumption and the production attributes of schooling. If schooling were altogether free, as already
remarked, a person would presumably consume of it until he
were satiated and "invest" in it until it would no longer increase his future earnings. If a part of the school expenditures
were borne on public account, the direct private costs would of
course be less than the total costs of schooling; and to the extent that such schooling increased the future earnings of the student, his private rate of return to what he spent on it would be
higher than the rate of return to total costs of the schooling entering into this part of his schooling. Thus, private incentives
to consume and to invest in schooling are affected by public expenditures, but the fact that there are such public expenditures
has no bearing on the question whether schooling is consumption
or investment in future earnings. That some schooling is compulsory is also irrelevant to the question at hand. To argue that
it applies is analogous to saying that a city ordinance which requires private owners of houses to install plumbing and sewage
disposal facilities is a factor in determining whether such facilities are a consumer or producer durable. Clearly, the compulsory
city ordinance does not provide a logical basis for distinguishing between these two types of durables.

The easy thing to do is, of course, to allocate none of the costs of schooling to consumption in studying the rate of return to schooling which show up in earnings. It avoids making an arbitrary allocation of costs between consumption and investment in such earnings, but it obviously overstates the real costs of the investment in skills and useful knowledge that students acquire in schools. Equally obvious, estimates of the rate of return based on all costs of schooling treated as the amount invested for this purpose are then too low. For example, if half of the cost of schooling were for consumption, an estimated rate of return of 9 percent based on total costs would be an 18 percent rate of return on that part of the costs incurred as a producer investment [100, sec. 9].

Weisbrod [78] puts the matter tersely: "Most economic analysis of return to education has focused on the contribution of education to earning capacity (and, presumably, to production capacity). While this has been valuable, it is only a part of the picture." A substantial part of his paper is devoted to those aspects of schooling "which increase welfare possibilities directly," some of which benefit the student and his family and some of which are captured by other individuals and families in the community. One of the merits of Weisbrod's analysis lies in the fact that the formal propositions on which he builds are based on concepts that presumably can be identified and measured.

The substance of the allocative problems under discussion bear directly on the key question: *Is there underinvestment in schooling?* Studies to ascertain the earnings that correspond to schooling and the rate of return to schooling that can be derived from such earnings are bringing new knowledge to bear on this question. But these studies do not answer the question. The concern expressed by Villard [76] is pertinent. Consider first the benefits of the favorable effects of schooling upon production capabilities: a part of them accrue to the student and a part is captured by others, for example, the "employment-related beneficiaries" considered by Weisbrod [78]. Literacy must have a pervasive value in improving the productivity of an economy. It must also be kept in mind that some of these benefits that accrue to the student do not become a part of earnings. Preparing one's own income tax return is a useful illustration [78]. The subsistence activities in agriculture could hide such benefits. Consider, next, the benefits of schooling that satisfy consumer preferences: here, also, they accrue in part to the student and his family and in part they are captured by others. Weisbrod's [78] resident-related beneficiaries is a way of classifying those consumer benefits that accrue to the current and future family of the student and to neighbors.

A Scale to Rate Schooling. Suppose, then, that all of the costs of schooling are charged to the investment in the production capabilities of students: What can be inferred from estimates of the rate of return based on this procedure? A great deal really, provided *the limits of the information* are always taken into account. Let me illustrate. In the case of a college education, when a rate of return based on total costs is as high as that on alternative investments, it follows that the greater the consumption component accruing to the student and his family and the greater the benefits captured by others, the larger the underinvestment. Moreover, it is possible to indicate a scale for rating different classes of schooling with regard to the students' consumption and with regard to the production and consumption benefits that accrue to others. In the case of elementary schooling, the rate of return derived from earnings is higher than that on alternative investments, and the consumption component accruing to the student and his family is large, and the benefits captured by others is, also, large. The three sets of contributions combined strongly support the inference that anything less than 8 years of schooling is a serious underinvestment.

It may be useful to elaborate briefly on a scale to rate schooling based on the criteria that have already been presented. Such a classification would differ from one country to another because of differences in earning prospects from schooling, costs of schooling, the organization of the economy, income of families, and differences in taste. In the United States presently, specific advanced schooling, that is, in law, agriculture, business, engineering, medicine, dentistry, nutrition, and technology, entails relatively little consumption and only a few of the benefits are captured by others. These classes are predominantly investments in productive capabilities that affect earnings and accrue to the persons who acquire the schooling. In the case of students who attend colleges which provide general programs of instruction and high school students who do not concentrate on vocational subjects, schooling contributes substantially to consumption, and the benefits captured by others are not small. As a working assumption, one half to three fifths of the costs of this schooling is invested in production capabilities that increase future earnings that accrue to students. Lastly, elementary schooling, as indicated above, is highly prized for its contribution to the consumption accruing to the student and his family. Elementary schooling has became an integral part of our standard of living viewed as a consumption component. It also generates a large set of production and consumption benefits that are captured by other individuals and families. Yet, in addition, its effects upon production capabilities which increase future earnings and which open doors for more schooling and subsequent on-the-job training are pronounced. No wonder, then, that we have long since opted for universal elementary education.

Rate of Return

It is essential to distinguish between the *return* and the *rate of return* for reasons already presented. It must be borne in mind that the *measured* return to schooling is simply that part of earnings attributed to education. Denison [90], it will be recalled, dealt exclusively with the return, that is, with the increases in real national income that are associated with additional schooling in the labor force. He had no reason to investigate the amount invested in schooling or the rate of return on whatever had been so invested.* But when the aim is to estimate the rate

---

*He faced one major difficulty, that is, what proportion of the observed differences in earnings associated with differences in schooling were the result of factors other than additional schooling. To cope with this difficulty, he made the assumption that "three-fifths of the reported income differentials represent differences in incomes from work *due to* differences in education as distinguished from associated characteristics." [90, p. 69]. What is important in this procedure is that it was not necessary for Denison, given his aim, to investigate either the amount invested or the rate of return to schooling.

of return, the important unsettled question is: What part of the costs of schooling is being invested in producer capabilities? The few studies that are at hand which attempt to estimate the rate of return to schooling assume, as a rule implicitly, that the amount invested is equal to the total costs of schooling.

Three Propositions about These Rates. Before turning to specific studies, I wish to propose three general propositions, which at this stage of our knowledge should be treated as hypotheses.

1. In *high* income countries, for example, in the United States, the rate of return to the costs of completing the 8 elementary grades is higher in general than is the rate of return to subsequent schooling. This proposition rests on: (1) the costs of elementary schooling are low mainly because at this level there are no earnings foregone (in the United States), whereas earnings foregone are large for schooling beyond the 8th grade;[†] and (2) the differences in earnings between those who complete elementary schooling and those who acquire more schooling, although they are large in absolute amounts and still imply a favorable return on the additional investment, are not large enough to produce on the much larger costs a rate equal to the high rate realized on what is invested upon completion of the elementary grades. Also, it should be noted that there are many indicators which show that the earning opportunities open to persons who have not completed 8 years of schooling are indeed meager, implying that the rate of return on, say, only 4 years of schooling is less than it is on the 8. A study by Hansen, [49] provides firm evidence supporting this implication.

2. A parallel proposition applicable to *low* income countries is necessarily more tentative because so little is known about

---

[†]Professor Burton A. Weisbrod in commenting on this proposition asks the following question: "Would you not agree that the relatively high foregone earnings of high school and college students reflect, at least in part, the high productivity of earlier education? That is, aside from physical maturity, the principle difference between a high school age person and a grade school age child is the additional education which the former may have had. Therefore, if foregone earnings for the older students were substantially higher than for the younger ones, this might well be some evidence of the effectiveness of the elementary education." (Quoted with permission.)

the key variables that enter. Thus, qualifications abound pertaining to whether there is work on farms or elsewhere that children can do, the seasonality of work and whether the peak season(s) overlap the school year, the structure of wages and salaries, and the state of information about them. Because of the heterogeneity among low income countries, let me restrict what follows to low income countries which have the growth and other relevant characteristics of Mexico. For these, the rate of return is high to the costs of completing the 6th grade of elementary schooling, based on differences in earnings of illiterate workers and workers who have completed the 6 years of elementary schooling. My reason for concentrating on the 6th year rather than the 8th year of schooling is that earnings foregone are already important in the 7th and 8th year of schooling in a country like Mexico. The underlying assumption is that schooling up to the age when earnings foregone enter into costs is highly "profitable" because the earning differentials referred to above are sufficiently large not only to offset the shorter expected working life span that is characteristic of low income countries, but in addition support a high rate of return. In formulating these propositions, all of the costs of schooling are implicitly charged against future earnings.

3. There is then the proposition that in high income countries, once adjustments are made for the consumption component in schooling and for the benefits that are captured by people other than the student and his family, the effects of such adjustments are to increase markedly the rate of return to elementary schooling relative to the rate realized on specialized advanced education. Assume, as is not unreasonable, that presently in the United States, at least one half and perhaps as much as two thirds of elementary schooling consists of consumption and benefits to others, whereas in the case of students attending schools for law, engineering, etc., only a small fraction of the benefits does not accrue to the students in earnings. The effect of adjustment in line with this assumption, obviously, is to raise substantially the rate of return to what is invested in elementary schooling relative to the rate of return realized on what is invested in advanced specialized education.

Bypassed Groups. It might be said, that inasmuch as elementary schooling is essentially universal in high income countries, the upper limit has been reached. In a number of countries with fairly homogeneous populations, in western Europe, northern Europe, and the United Kingdom, there is in fact universal elementary schooling, and it is in general high in quality. In the United States, however, despite the high level of income, some people, notably many Negroes, Mexican nationals, families of migratory laborers, and some "poor whites," are receiving less than 8 years of elementary schooling, and what they receive is frequently far below par in quality. There is, also, a strong presumption with respect to many countries that are thought of as being quite poor that the best "pay-off" in terms of production and earnings to people is in more and better elementary schooling. The data for Venezuela, to which I now turn, support this presumption.

Estimates for Venezuela. Shoup and associates [73] estimate that the incremental return to investment in primary schooling in Venezuela is between 82 and 130 percent per annum. Presumably the data are for 1957-58. A 10 percent rate is used in accumulating the costs of the 6 years that enter into primary schooling. The lower rate of return is based on incremental earnings of a primary school graduate over an illiterate urban worker, and the higher rate is that over an illiterate agricultural worker. For secondary schooling, the 7th through the 11th year of schooling, when earnings foregone make up most of the costs, the rate of return is 17 percent; and, for the 4 years of university schooling, a rate of 23 percent is shown. In each of these estimates, the total costs of schooling is allocated to investment in these earning capabilities.

Estimates for Israel. In the Klinov-Malul [41] study of the "Profitability of Investment in Education in Israel," based on cross-section data of the average annual income of heads of families from employment by level of education, standardized to adjust for country of origin and length of residence, it was found that the rate of return to the completion (8 years) of elementary schooling is about 17 percent. This estimate is for 1957-58. In Israel, 18 percent of the total costs of this schooling consisted of earnings foregone. The estimated rate of return to the additional four years required to complete the secondary school is only 6.5 percent. There are according to this study some special circumstances in the unique pattern of the population associated with past in-migration that explain the low rate of return reported [41, see p. 143]. Earnings foregone are about three fifths of the total costs of secondary schooling. Here, too, all costs are charged to the investment in earning capabilities; none are charged to consumption or to benefits captured by people other than the student and his family.

The 1957-58 rates of return to higher education in Israel [41, Table 2, p. 144] based on *total costs,* as reported by the Klinov-Malul, are: When work is for a wage or salary, physicians, 4 percent, engineers and lawyers, 8 percent; when self-employed, the rates are 3, 14, and 20 percent respectively. Auditors must have enjoyed a boom, earning "50 + percent." The rates of return to the costs that individuals bear are much higher, for example, engineers self-employed, 30 percent, lawyers self-employed, 25 percent, and physicians working for a salary, 25 percent.

Estimates for the United States. These are some preliminary estimates by Becker [30], Hansen [49], Gisser [44], and myself [19]. Against total costs, including earnings foregone, for white urban males, the rate of return to a college education came to 9 percent according to Becker. This estimate is for 1940 and 1950 before tax, adjusted for ability, race, unemployment, and mortality. For 4 years of high school, as of 1939, the estimate was 14.3 percent [19, p. 78]. From changes in lifetime earnings for all males associated with schooling to costs of such schooling [19, Table 17], the rate of return to a college education rose substantially between 1939 and 1958 and that to 4 years of high school declined markedly between 1939 and 1949, after which it rose appreciably. The 1958 data appear to support the following rates of return: elementary, 35 percent; high school, 10 percent; and college, 11 percent [19, Table 18]. Based on internal rates of return to total resource investment in schooling, Hansen's estimates [49] for males, 1949, show that the marginal rate of return rises rapidly from the completion of the first 2 years to the completion of the 7th and 8th years of schooling, from a rate of about 9 to 29 percent. This marginal rate of return then declines for high school and college; the 11th and 12th year of schooling show a return of nearly 14 percent and the 15th and 16th year a strong 15 percent. Gisser's study [44] implies a high rate of return to schooling even for hired farm workers in the United States, a finding which comes as a surprise. It had not been known that differences in wages to farm workers were as large as they are and that a considerable part of these differences are related to differences in schooling.

IV. THE UNFINISHED SEARCH

At the outset of this essay, three basic matters in economics about which investigators have been puzzled were introduced. It was then proposed that investment in human capital, of which schooling is a large part, is a key factor in each of these matters.

1. Based on the assumption that the fundamental motives and preferences which determine the ratio of *all* capital to income remain essentially constant, the hypothesis here advanced is that the inclusion of human capital will show that the ratio of *all* capital to income is not declining. Producer goods – structures, equipment, and inventories – a particular stock of capital, has been declining relative to income.[†] Meanwhile, however, the stock of human capital has been rising relative to income [102]. Have the underlying decisions that account for this shift been motivated by differences in the rates of return? The key, however, is: If the ratio of *all* capital to income remains essentially constant, then the unexplained economic growth, discussed at some length in this essay, originates out of forms of capital that have not been identified and measured and consists mainly of human capital.

2. The next critical assumption is that the economic capabilities of man are predominantly a *produced means of production* and that, except for some pure rent (in earnings) for differences in inherited abilities, most of the differences in earnings are a

---

[†]Simon Kuznets, assisted by Elizabeth Jenks, *Capital in the American Economy: Its Formation and Financing.* (A study of the National Bureau of Economic Research.) Princeton: Princeton University Press, 1961.

consequence of differences in the amounts that have been invested in people. The implication of this assumption is that the structure of wages and salaries, which has long baffled economists, is determined in the long run by investment in schooling, health, on-the-job training, and in searching for information about job opportunities, and in acting on it. To cope analytically with investment in people, Becker's [29] formulation becomes a rich source of hypothesis. The findings of Mincer [60], pursuing one of these leads, indicate that the investment in on-the-job training strongly supports the assumption made here. So does the investment in schooling. Thus, there is a logical and empirical basis to explain the structure of wages and salaries.

3. In analyzing the personal distribution of income, based on the assumption that the rise in the investment in human capital relative to that invested in nonhuman capital increases earnings relative to property income, and that the more equal distribution of investments in man equalize earnings among human agents, the hypothesis here proposed is that these changes in the investment in human capital are a basic factor reducing the inequality in the personal distribution of income. One of the implications of this formulation is that changes in income transfers, in progressive taxation, and changes in the distribution of privately owned wealth have been overrated as factors in altering the personal distribution of income. Will the underlying facts support this hypothesis? If they do, what part have private savings and sacrifices of mature students and of their parents and of workers training on-the-job played, and what part have public funds and private grants played in this equalization process?

Turning next to unresolved issues that bear directly on schooling and the educational establishment, those relating to costs have already been presented in Chapter II under the heading "Some Unsettled Questions Pertaining to Costs." Thus, it will not be necessary to elaborate on them here. A brief reference will suffice.

4. The scope of schooling requires more attention than it has received. Machlup's [212] classification of the sources of education as a part of the production and distribution of knowledge has merit. The conception used by Blitz [2] is also relevant.

5. When schools receive special tax treatment, are such taxes which public taxing bodies forego one of the costs of schooling? The logic for including some and excluding others is briefly examined by Weisbrod [78].

6. The state of knowledge of who bears the cost of schooling is most unsatisfactory. In part this is true because of the neglect of earnings foregone in reckoning these costs. In part, however, it is a consequence of the fact that in public finance, to the best of my knowledge, local school taxes are not analyzed in accordance with the "benefits received theory" applied to particular taxes that provide improvements which enhance the value of the property on which the taxes are assessed. Nor have "gifts" by parents to support parochial schools been examined in this connection.

7. The assumption that earnings foregone are a key explanatory variable of a large set of behavior observed empirically implies a major hypothesis waiting to be tested. Are the differences between earnings foregone that are borne by workers who enter upon training on-the-job and those borne by students while attending school the explanation for the observed shifts from learning on-the-job to learning in school [60]? Is it, also, the key to why farm children attend school less than do urban children? Or, in explaining why many talented children from low income homes, even when tuition is free or scholarships to cover tuition are provided, do not avail themselves of the additional educational opportunities? Are there earnings foregone even at ages 10 or 12 in particular low income countries, and if so, do these sacrifices explain why many children in such countries are not continuing their schooling after completing 4 or 5 grades?

8. The exact general relations between earnings foregone, level of family income, and earning opportunities, present and prospective, await formulation. Identification and measurement problems abound.

The hard core of what is unfinished, more accurately, the part of the search just begun, pertains to the *economic value of education.* A number of the basic problems waiting to be resolved have been presented in Chapter III. What is said here can, therefore, be very brief.

9. One half of the basic research underway in the United States is within the educational establishment [138]. Suppose it is a quest for knowledge for its own sake; nevertheless, much of the new knowledge becomes valuable in what it contributes to real national income. That economic growth is affected favorably is not in doubt. What is not known is the approximate magnitude of these benefits and what they imply as a *rate* of return on the expenditures for this research.

10. Nowhere have economists come to grips with the basic factors that determine the growth in demand for human agents with skills and knowledge associated with schooling. Is this growth in the demand for high-level capabilities in labor specific to our economy? Or, is it also to be observed in particular low income countries? It is hard to believe that the demand for these quality components in labor increased rapidly during the early industrialization in western Europe. Labor was then abundant and "cheap"; it was mainly illiterate and unskilled; and it did mostly manual work that required much brute force. Improvements in skills and knowledge and health of workers generally appear not to have been a prerequisite to the impressive economic growth of that period [68].

Despite a flood of schooling beyond the elementary grades entering the labor market, the earning differentials in favor of workers with such schooling imply that the *rate* of return to it has not been beaten down.* It appears to have risen somewhat during the last decade.† Meanwhile, workers who had completed 1 to 4 years of high school rose from 38 to 52 percent, and those

---

*Except perhaps for high school between 1939 and 1949.

†Professor Burton W. Weisbrod suggests the following hypothesis: "Through time, living standards have risen, population has shifted from the farms to urban areas, and it has become increasingly easy for students to attend public colleges while living at home; these factors have probably opened the doors of education at all levels to able students who previously could not attend schools for financial reasons. My conclusion is that the average quality of the student body has improved through time. This would be sufficient explanation for the apparent maintenance of rates of return on education costs." (Quoted with permission.)

with some college (completed 1 to more than 4 years) rose from
about 13 to 19 percent of the U. S. labor force between 1940 and
1958.** If the rate of return had fallen sharply as a consequence
of this flood, it might be argued that the demand for these capabilities had not shifted so much to the right since they were
being priced lower down on the demand schedule. But this seems
not to have happened except for a short period for high school.
Therefore, the same hard question: What factors account for the
high rate of growth in the demand for these capabilities of
schooling beyond the 8th grade?

11. It will not suffice to treat the total costs of schooling as
if the only benefit from schooling were increases in future earnings. No doubt it will be hard to untangle the skein of benefits
of schooling. Which of the threads is consumption? When does
this consumption accrue to the student and his family and when
is it captured by others? Of the part that becomes an investment
in the student's capabilities, how much accrues to the student in
earnings and in other ways? How much of it goes to other individuals and families? Here it will be necessary to break the
analysis down into relatively homogeneous units of schooling by
countries classified by level of income, earning opportunities,
costs of schooling, and other relevant variables in order to make
the task manageable. There is much to be said for treating
grades 1 to 4, 5 to 7, and the 8th separately, and so on up. In
low income countries, an even finer classification may be required. It is not so much the logical basis of distinguishing
among the benefits of schooling that is beset with difficulties as
it is to identify and to measure them.†

**Percent distribution by years of school completed for the labor
force 18 to 64 years old. *Statistical Abstract of the United States, 1960,*
Table 139. Inasmuch as the length of the school year has been increasing, these estimates understate to this extent the rise in real schooling. There is some upward bias in the reports on which these estimates
are based. Whether it has changed over time is not evident.

†Professor W. Lee Hansen in commenting on this section observed
(quoted with permission) "(1) Again, the differences in the situation of
females needs to be investigated. (2) Also, if we are to think of educational investment as a source of growth, it will soon become necessary
to rethink some of our traditional national income accounting concepts
so as to incorporate this new formulation. (3) What about the obsoles-

12. What do schooling and the acquisition of knowledge from abroad contribute to the economic growth of low income countries? The hypothesis implied in Horvat's [53] formulation of the optimum rate of investment which treats schooling and knowledge as critical investment variables needs to be tested. The experience of a number of countries, for example, Denmark from 1870 to 1900 [185], Mexico since 1930 [3, 162, 175], Japan [13, 120], Israel [41], and the Soviet Union [112], is relevant, so it would appear in undertaking such a test.

Lastly, there are unresolved problems not explored in this essay. Of these two will be mentioned.

13. To what extent do tax laws discriminate against human capital, specifically against investment in schooling? Like other forms of reproducible capital, it depreciates, becomes obsolete, and entails maintenance. Our tax laws are blind on these matters [67]. It is true that earnings foregone do not go through the personal income accounts and thus no income tax is paid on them. A study by Goode [116] of educational expenditures and the income tax provides the analytical basis on which others will want to build.

14. How satisfactorily does the capital market function in providing funds to students to invest in their schooling? The general belief is that this side of the capital market is highly imperfect. On the other hand, some colleges have some funds to loan to students. It is often alleged that students are not in the "market" for these funds to the extent that they exhaust them. Various new bank loans for students are being introduced. Abroad, Sweden has had considerable experience in providing loans to students. Also, there are now federal funds for this purpose. All of these experiences as well as the functioning of the capital market generally with respect to investment in schooling awaits analysis.

An unfinished search is always facing unknowns. There is no royal road. The right questions to pursue are among the unknowns in this game.

cence of human knowledge and skills, or human capital. With a rapid rate of technological change and a continuous revolution in the state of our knowledge, the education of 20 years ago may not be worth much if it has not been maintained or if adequate on-the-job training has not provided new and better skills."

SELECTED BIBLIOGRAPHY

I. Costs of Education

1. Abramovitz, Moses, and Vera Eliasberg. *The Growth of Public Employment in Great Britain.* (National Bureau of Economic Research General Series, No. 60.) Princeton: Princeton University Press, 1957.
2. Blitz, Rudolph. "The Nation's Educational Outlay," in *The Economics of Higher Education,* ed. Selma J. Mushkin. Washington: U. S. Department of Health, Education, and Welfare, Office of Education, 1962.
3. Carnoy, Martin. "Cost of Education in Mexico." (University of Chicago, Department of Economics, Economics of Education Research Paper, No. 61-8.) 1961. (Mimeographed.)
4. Clark, H. F., and H. S. Sloan. *Classrooms in the Factories.* New York: New York University Press, 1955, Chapter 4.
5. *The Cost of a Schoolhouse; a Report.* New York: Educational Facilities Laboratories, Inc., 1960.
6. Deitch, Kenneth. "Some Observations on the Allocation of Resources in Higher Education," *Review of Economics and Statistics* (supplement), XLII (August, 1960), 192-99.
7. Edding, Friedrich. *Internationale Tendenzen in der Entwicklung der Ausgaben für Schulen und Hochschulen.* (Forschungsberichte des Instituts für Weltwirtschaft und der Universität Kiel, 47.) Kiel: Kieler Studien, 1958.
8. Fabricant, Solomon. *The Trend of Government Activity in the United States Since 1900.* New York: National Bureau of Economic Research, 1952.
9. Folsom, Marion B. "Some Suggested Adjustments in the Use of Our Resources," *Proceedings of the American Philosophical Society* (Philadelphia), CII (August, 1958), 321-27.
10. Harris, Seymour E. "Education as a Demand on Resources Competing with Other Activities," in *Yearbook of Educa-*

tion, 1956, eds. R. K. Hall and J. A. Lauwery. London: Evans Brothers, 1956.

11. — *More Resources for Education.* (The John Dewey Society Lectureship Series, No. 3.) New York: Harper and Brothers, 1960.

12. Hirsch, Z. *Analysis of the Rising Costs of Public Education.* Congressional Joint Economic Committee, 86th Congress, 1st Session. Washington: U. S. Government Printing Office, 1959.

13. Japan, Government of. *Education in 1956.* The Annual Report of the Ministry of Education. Japan: Ministry of Education, Research Bureau, Research Section, March, 1958.

14. Kershaw, Joseph A., and Roland N. McKean. *Systems Analysis and Education.* (RM–2473–FF.) Santa Monica: The RAND Corporation, October 30, 1959.

15. Martin, Allison M., and W. A. Lewis. "Patterns of Public Revenue and Expenditure," *Manchester School of Economic and Social Studies* (Manchester), XXIV (September, 1956), 203-44.

16. Rude, Robert. "Assets of Private Nonprofit Institutions in the United States, 1890-1948." A Preliminary Draft of a Proposed Occasional Paper of the National Bureau of Economic Research, 1954. (Mimeographed.)

17. Ruml, Beardsley, and Sidney G. Tickton. *Teaching Salaries, Then and Now.* (Bulletin No. 1.) New York: Fund for the Advancement of Education, 1956.

18. Schultz, Theodore W. "Capital Formation by Education," *Journal of Political Economy,* LXVIII (December, 1960), 571-83.

19. — "Education and Economic Growth," in *Social Forces Influencing American Education,* ed. Nelson B. Henry. Chicago: University of Chicago Press, 1961.

20. Stigler, George J. *Employment and Compensation in Education.* (National Bureau of Economic Research. Occasional Paper, No. 33.) New York, 1950.

21. Tarver, J. D. "Costs of Rearing and Educating Farm Children," *Journal of Farm Economics,* XXXVIII (February, 1956), 144-53.

22. Tickton, Sidney G. *Teaching Salaries Then and Now – A Second Look.* New York: The Fund for the Advancement of Education, 1961.
23. United States, Government of. Department of Health, Education, and Welfare. *Costs of Attending College.* (Office of Education, Bulletin, No. 9.) Washington: U. S. Government Printing Office, 1957.
24. — *Indicators.* Washington: U. S. Government Printing Office, September, 1961.
25. — *Trends.* Annual Supplement, 1961. Washington: U. S. Government Printing Office, 1961.
26. Vaizey, John. *The Costs of Education.* London: Allen and Unwin, 1958.
27. Wang, T. N. "Some Problems of International Comparison of Public Social Expenditures," *Indian Economic Review* (Delhi), II (February, 1955), 23-52.

II. Economic Value of Schooling

A. *Investment in Human Capital, Earnings, and Return to Education*

28. Ashby, Sir Eric. *Investment in Education: The Report of the Commission on Post-School Certificate and Higher Education in Nigeria.* Nigeria: Federal Ministry of Education, 1960.
29. Becker, Gary S. "Investment in Human Capital: A Theoretical Analysis," *Journal of Political Economy* (supplement), LXX (October, 1962).
30. — "Underinvestment in Education?" *American Economic Review,* L (May, 1960), 346-54.
31. Bowman, Mary Jean. "Human Capital: Concepts and Measures," in *The Economics of Higher Education,* ed. Selma J. Mushkin. Washington: U. S. Department of Health, Education, and Welfare, Office of Education, 1962.
32. Bowman, Mary Jean, and C. Arnold Anderson. "The Role of Education in Development," in *Development of the Emerging Countries,* pp. 153-80. Washington, D.C.: The Brookings Institution, February, 1962.

33. Bridgman, D. S. "Problems in Estimating the Monetary Value of College Education," *Review of Economics and Statistics,* XLII (August, 1960).
34. Clark, H. F. "The Return on Educational Investment," in *Yearbook of Education, 1956,* eds. R. K. Hall and J. A. Lauwery, pp. 495-506. London: Evans Brothers, 1956.
35. Dalton, Hugh. *Some Aspects of the Inequality of Income in Modern Communities.* London: Routledge, 1920.
36. Dublin, L. I., and A. J. Lotka. *The Money Value of a Man.* (Revised ed.) New York: Ronald Press, 1946.
37. Eckaus, R. S. "On the Comparison of Human Capital and Physical Capital." Center for International Studies, Massachusetts Institute of Technology, Economic Development Program, 1961. (Mimeographed.)
38. Eicher, Jean-Claude. "The Problem of Investment in Education." (University of Chicago, Department of Economics, Economics of Education Research Paper, No. 59-1.) 1959. (Mimeographed.)
39. Ellis, A. Caswell. "The Money Value of Education," *Bureau of Education, Bulletin, 1917,* No. 22. Washington: U. S. Department of the Interior, 1917.
40. *Evidence of Employers of Labourers on the Influence of Training and Education on the Value of Workmen, and on the Comparative Eligibility of Educated and Uneducated Workmen for Employment.* London: Printed by W. Clowes and Sons for Her Majesty's Stationery Office, 1840.
41. *The Falk Project for Economic Research in Israel; Fifth Report; 1959 and 1960,* pp. 138-46, and 146-50. Jerusalem, 1961.
42. Friedman, Milton, and Simon Kuznets. *Income from Independent Professional Practice.* (Publications of the National Bureau of Economic Research, No. 45.) New York, 1945.
43. Ginzberg, Eli. "How Men Acquire Skills," *Employment Security Review,* June, 1955.
44. Gisser, Micha. Schooling and the Agricultural Labor Force. A Ph. D. dissertation in economics, University of Chicago, October, 1962. Unpublished.
45. Glick, Paul C., and Herman P. Miller. "Educational Level

SELECTED BIBLIOGRAPHY
75

and Potential Income," *American Sociological Review,* XXI (June, 1956), 307-12.

46. Goode, R. "Adding to the Stock of Physical and Human Capital," *American Economic Review,* XLIX (May, 1959), 147-55.

47. Grunfeld, Yehuda. "The Measurement of Human Capital in Israel." A draft report prepared for the Falk Project for Economic Research in Israel. Jerusalem, 1961. (Mimeographed.)

48. Haavelmo, Trygve. *A Study in the Theory of Investment.* Chicago: University of Chicago Press, 1960.

49. Hansen, W. Lee. "Total and Private Rates of Return to Investment in Schooling," *Journal of Political Economy.* LXXI (April, 1963).

50. Harberger, A. C. "Using the Resources at Hand More Effectively," *American Economic Review,* XLIX (May, 1959), 134-46.

51. Harbison, Frederick. "High-Level Manpower for Nigeria's Future," in *Investment in Education,* Federal Ministry of Education, Nigeria, 1960.

52. Hayek, F. A. "The Use of Knowledge in Society," *American Economic Review,* XXXV (September, 1945), 519-30.

53. Horvat, S. "The Optimum Rate of Investment," *Economic Journal,* LXVIII (December, 1958), 747-67.

54. Houthakker, H. S. "Education and Income," *Review of Economics and Statistics,* XLI (February, 1959), 24-28.

55. Kapp, Friedrich. *Immigration and the Commissioners of Emigration of the State of New York.* New York: The Nation Press, 1870.

56. Keat, P. "Long Term Trends in Occupational Wage Differentials," *Journal of Political Economy,* LXVIII (December, 1960), 584-600.

57. Marshall, Alfred. *Principles of Economics.* 8th ed., pp. 193-239, and 546-79. London: Macmillan and Company, 1925.

58. Miller, Herman P. "Annual and Lifetime Income in Relation to Education, 1939-1959," *American Economic Review,* L (December, 1960), 962-86.

59. Mincer, Jacob. "Investment in Human Capital and Personal

Distribution of Income," *Journal of Political Economy,* LXVI (August, 1958), 281-302.

60. — "On the Job Training: Costs, Returns and Some Implications," *Journal of Political Economy* (supplement), LXX (October, 1962).

61. Muhsam, H. "Revision of the Concept—The Money Value of a Man," in *International Population Conference.* pp. 106-10. Vienna: International Union for the Scientific Study of Population, 1959.

62. Mushkin, Selma J., ed. *The Economics of Higher Education.* Washington: U. S. Department of Health, Education, and Welfare, Office of Education, 1962.

63. Nicholson, J. S. "The Living Capital of the United Kingdom," *Economic Journal,* I (March, 1891), 95-107.

64. Renshaw, E. F. "Estimating the Returns to Education," *Review of Economics and Statistics,* XLII (August, 1960), 318-24.

65. Schultz, Theodore W. "A Critique of U. S. Endeavors to Assist Low Income Countries Improve the Economic Capabilities of Their People," *Journal of Farm Economics,* XLIII (December, 1961), 1068-77.

66. — "Human Capital: A Growing Asset Inside the Soviet Economy," *Saturday Review,* January 21, 1961.

67. — "Investment in Human Capital," *American Economic Review,* LI (March, 1961), pp. 1-17.

68. — "Investment in Human Capital in Poor Countries," J. E. Owens Memorial Foundation Lecture. *Foreign Trade and Human Capital,* ed. Paul D. Zook. Southern Methodist University, 1962.

69. — "Investment in Human Capital: Reply," *American Economic Review,* LI (December, 1961), 1035-39.

70. — "Investment in Man: An Economist's View," *Social Service Review,* XXXIII (June, 1959), 110-17.

71. — "Rise in the Capital Stock Represented by Education in the United States between 1900 to 1957," in *The Economics of Higher Education,* ed. Selma J. Mushkin. Washington: U. S. Department of Health, Education and Welfare, Office of Education, 1962.

72. Shaffer, Harry G. "Investment in Human Capital: Comment," *American Economic Review,* LI (December, 1961), 1026-35.
73. Shoup, Carl S., et. al. *The Fiscal System of Venezuela.* A Report of the Commission to Study the Fiscal System of Venezuela. Baltimore: The Johns Hopkins Press, 1959.
74. Soltow, L. "The Distribution of Income Related to Changes in the Distribution of Education, Age and Occupation," *Review of Economics and Statistics,* XLII (November, 1960), 450-53.
75. Staehle, H. "Ability, Wages and Income," *Review of Economics and Statistics,* XXV (February, 1943), 77-87.
76. Villard, H. H. " 'Discussion' of Becker's 'Underinvestment in College Education?' " *American Economic Review, Papers and Proceedings,* L (May, 1960), 375-78.
77. Walsh, J. "Capital Concept Applied to Man," *Quarterly Journal of Economics* (Cambridge), XLIX (February, 1935), 255-85.
78. Weisbrod, Burton A. "Education and the Investment in Human Capital," *Journal of Political Economy* (supplement), LXX (October, 1962).
79. — "The Valuation of Human Capital," *Journal of Political Economy,* LXIX (October, 1961), 425-36.
80. Wiles, P. J. D. "The Nation's Intellectual Investment," *Bulletin of the Oxford University Institute of Statistics,* XVIII (August, 1956), 279-90.
81. Wolfle, Dael Lee. *America's Resources of Specialized Talent; A Current Appraisal and a Look Ahead.* A Report to the Commission on Human Resources and Advanced Training. New York: Harper, 1954.
82. — "Economics and Educational Values," *Review of Economics and Statistics* (supplement), XLII (August, 1960).
83. Wolfle, Dael Lee, and Joseph G. Smith. "The Occupational Value of Education for Superior High-School Graduates," *Journal of Higher Education,* XXVII (April, 1956), 201-13.
84. Woods, E. A., and C. B. Metzger. *America's Human Wealth; the Money Value of Human Life.* New York: Crofts and Co., 1927.
85. Zeman, Morton. A Quantitative Analysis of White-Nonwhite

Income Differentials in the U. S. Unpublished dissertation. Chicago: University of Chicago, 1955.

B. Education, a Source of Economic Growth

86. Abramovitz, M. "Resource and Output Trends in the United States Since 1870," *American Economic Review*, XLVI (May, 1956), 5-23. Reprinted as Occasional Paper 52, National Bureau of Economic Research. New York, 1956.
87. Aukrust, O. "Investment and Economic Growth," *Productivity Measurement Review* (Paris, OEEC), 16 (February, 1959), 35-50.
88. Aukrust, O., and J. Bjerke. "Real Capital and Economic Growth in Norway, 1900-56," in *Conference on Research on Income and Wealth, Series VIII*, eds. R. Goldsmith and C. Saunders. Cambridge: Bowes and Bowes, 1959.
89. Denison, Edward F. "Education, Economic Growth, and Gaps in Information," *Journal of Political Economy* (supplement), LXX (October, 1962).
90. — *The Sources of Economic Growth in the United States and the Alternatives Before Us*. New York: Committee for Economic Development, 1962.
91. Eckaus, R. S. "Education and Economic Growth," in *The Economics of Higher Education*, ed. Selma J. Mushkin. Washington: U. S. Department of Health, Education, and Welfare, Office of Education, 1962.
92. Hagen, E. E. "How Economic Growth Begins: A General Theory Applied to Japan," *Public Opinion Quarterly*, XXII (No. 3, 1958).
93. Kuznets, Simon. *Six Lectures on Economic Growth*. Glencoe, Illinois: Free Press, 1959.
94. — "Toward a Theory of Economic Growth," in *National Policy for Economic Welfare at Home and Abroad*, ed. R. Leckachman. New York: Doubleday, 1955.
95. Leibenstein, H. *Economic Backwardness and Economic Growth*. New York: John Wiley and Sons, Inc., 1957.
96. — "Underemployment in Backward Economies: Some Additional Notes," *Journal of Political Economy*, LXVI (June, 1958), 256-258.

97. Lewis, W. Arthur. *The Theory of Economic Growth*. Homewood, Illinois: Irwin, 1955.
98. Organisation for Economic Co-Operation and Development. *Policy Conference on Economic Growth and Investment in Education*. Conference held in Washington, D. C., October 16-20, 1961. Published in five parts. Paris, 1962.
99. Rosovsky, Henry. *Capital Formation in Japan, 1868-1940*. New York: The Free Press of Glencoe, 1961.
100. Schultz, Theodore W. "Education as a Source of Economic Growth." Paper presented at a conference sponsored by ECLA, OAS, and UNESCO in Santiago, Chile, March, 1962.
101. — "Human Wealth and Economic Growth," *The Humanist* (No. 2), 1959.
102. — "Reflections on Investment in Man," *Journal of Political Economy* (supplement), LXX (October, 1962).

III. Demand, Supply, Adjustments, and Policy

103. Anderson, C. Arnold, James C. Brown, and Mary Jean Bowman. "Intelligence and Occupational Mobility," *Journal of Political Economy*, LX (June, 1952), 218-39.
104. Benson, Charles S., and Paul R. Lohnes. "Public Education and the Development of Work Skills," *Harvard Educational Review*, XXIX (Spring, 1959), 137-50.
105. — "Skill Requirements and Industrial Training in Durable Goods Manufacturing," *Industrial and Labor Relations Review*, XII (July, 1959), 540-53.
106. Blank, David, and George J. Stigler. *The Demand and Supply of Scientific Personnel*. (National Bureau of Economic Research General Series, No. 62). New York, 1957.
107. Brazer, Harvey E. *City Expenditures in the United States*. Occasional Paper No. 66. New York: National Bureau of Economic Research, 1959.
108. Brown, J. Douglas, and Frederick Harbison. *High-Talent Manpower for Science and Industry*. An Appraisal of Policies at Home and Abroad. (Princeton University, Department of Economics and Sociology, Industrial Relations Section, Research Reports Series, No. 95.) 1957.

109. Clark, Noble. "Education Must Come First," *Educational Record*, 30 (April, 1949), 179-85.
110. Committee for Economic Development. *Paying for Better Public Schools; a Statement of National Policy by the Research and Policy Committee of the C. E. D.* New York: Committee for Economic Development, 1959.
111. Cremin, Lawrence A. *The Transformation of the School; Progressivism in American Education, 1876-1957.* New York: Alfred A. Knopf, 1961.
112. DeWitt, Nicholas. *Soviet Professional Manpower, Its Education, Training, and Supply.* Washington: National Science Foundation, 1955.
113. Floud, J. E., and A. H. Halsey. "Education and Occupation: English Secondary Schools and the Supply of Labour," in *Year Book of Education, 1956,* pp. 519-32. Yonkers: World Book Company, 1956.
114. Friedman, Milton. "The Role of Government in Education," in *Economics and the Public Interest,* ed. Robert A. Solo, pp. 123-44. New Brunswick: Rutgers University Press, 1955.
115. Goode, Richard. "Educational Expenditures and the Income Tax," in *The Economics of Higher Education,* ed. Selma J. Mushkin. Washington: U. S. Department of Health, Education, and Welfare, Office of Education, 1962.
116. — "The Income Tax and the Supply of Labor," *Journal of Political Economy,* LVII (October, 1949), 428-37.
117. Hansen, W. Lee. "The 'Shortage' of Engineers," *Review of Economics and Statistics,* XLIII (August, 1961), 251-56.
118. Heady, Earl O. "Public Purpose in Agricultural Research and Education," *Journal of Farm Economics,* XLIII (August, 1961), 566-81.
119. Hirsch, Werner Z. "Determinants of Public Education Expenditures," *National Tax Journal,* XIII (March, 1960).
120. Japan, Government of. *Demand and Supply for University Graduates.* Japan: Ministry of Education, Research Bureau, Research Section, August, 1958.
121. Johnson, Harry G. "The Political Economy of Opulence," *Canadian Journal of Economics and Political Science,* 26 (November, 1960), 552-64.

122. Kapp, Friedrich. (See II-A above.)
123. Melby, John F. "The Rising Demand for International Education," *The Annals of the American Academy of Political and Social Science,* 335 (May, 1961).
124. Morse, John F. *An Aid to Administrators of National Defense Student Loans.* New York: College Entrance Examination Board, 1959.
125. National Manpower Council. *Improving the Work Skills of the Nation.* New York: Columbia University Press, 1955.
126. — *A Policy for Scientific and Professional Manpower.* New York: Columbia University Press, 1953.
127. Platt, William J. *Toward Strategies of Education.* Menlo Park, California: International Industrial Development Center, Stanford Research Institute, 1961.
128. Rivlin, Alice M. *The Role of the Federal Government in Financing Higher Education.* Washington: The Brookings Institution, 1961.
129. Rottenberg, S. "The Economics of Occupational Licensing." A paper read before the National Bureau of Economic Research Conference on Labor Economics, April, 1960.
130. Schultz, Theodore W. "The Emerging Economic Scene and Its Relations to High-School Education," in *The High School in a New Era,* eds. F. S. Chase and H. A. Anderson. Chicago: University of Chicago Press, 1958.
131. — "A Policy to Redistribute Losses from Economic Progress," in *Labor Mobility and Population in Agriculture.* Ames: Iowa State College Press, 1961.
132. — "The Role of Government in Promoting Economic Growth," in *The State of the Social Sciences,* eds. F. S. Chase and H. A. Anderson. Chicago: University of Chicago Press, 1958.
133. Shapiro, Sherman. An Analysis of the Determinants of Current Public and Societal Expenditures Per Pupil in Elementary and Secondary Schools, Decennially, 1920-1950. A Ph. D. dissertation in economics, University of Chicago, April, 1962. Unpublished.
134. Stigler, George J. "The Economics of Information," *Journal of Political Economy,* LXIX (June, 1961), 213-25.

135. — "Information in the Labor Market," *Journal of Political Economy* (supplement), LXX (October, 1962).

136. United States, Government of. Department of Labor. *Training and Retraining in Depressed Areas.* (U. S. Department of Labor, Bulletin, No. T-152.) Washington: U. S. Government Printing Office, 1961.

137. — National Education Association. *Teacher Supply and Demand in Universities, Colleges, and Junior Colleges, 1957-58 and 1958-59; a Study.* (Higher Education Research Report, No. 1959-R10.) Washington: U. S. Government Printing Office, 1959.

138. — National Science Foundation. *Investing in Scientific Progress, 1961-1970; Concepts, Goals, and Projections.* Washington: U. S. Government Printing Office, 1961.

139. Van Den Haag, Ernest. *Education as an Industry.* New York: Augustus M. Kelley, 1956.

140. Wiseman, J. "The Economics of Education," *Scottish Journal of Political Economy* (Edinburgh), VI (February, 1959), 48-58.

141. Youmans, Grant. *The Educational Attainment and Future Plans of Kentucky Rural Youths.* (University of Kentucky, Kentucky Agricultural Experiment Station Bulletin, No. 664.) 1959.

IV. Education in Social and Economic Development

142. Anderson, C. Arnold. "The Impact of the Educational System on Technological Change and Modernization." Paper presented at the North American Conference on the Social Implications of Industrialization and Technological Change, sponsored by UNESCO, in Chicago, Illinois, September 15-22, 1960.

143. Ashby, Sir Eric. *Technology and the Academics.* London: Macmillan and Co. Ltd., 1958.

144. Banfield, Edward C. *The Moral Basis of a Backward Society.* New York: The Free Press of Glencoe, 1958.

145. Bauer, P., and B. Yaney. *The Economics of Under-Developed Countries.* (The Cambridge Economic Handbooks Se-

ries.) Chicago: University of Chicago Press, 1957.
146. Benham, F. C. "Education and Economic Development in the Under-Developed Countries," *International Affairs* (London), XXXV (April, 1959), 181-87.
147. Bowman, Mary Jean, and C. Arnold Anderson. "Concerning the Role of Education in Development," in *Old Societies and New States*, ed. C. Geertz. London: Free Press of Glencoe, 1963.
148. — *Human Resource Development and Economic Development.* Chicago: University of Chicago, Comparative Education Center, May, 1961. (Mimeographed.)
149. — "The Role of Education in Development," in *Development of the Emerging Countries,* pp. 153-80. Washington, D. C.: The Brookings Institution, February, 1962.
150. Carnegie Endowment Study Group. "Needs and Resources for Social Investment," (discussion in Geneva, 1959), *International Social Science Journal,* XII(3) (1960), 409-33.
151. Cotgrave, Stephen F. *Technical Education and Social Change.* London: Ruskin House, 1958.
152. Debeauvais, Michel, and John Vaizey. "Some Economic Aspects of Educational Development in Europe," in "Report of the Proceedings of a Conference held at the Villa Serbelloni, Bellagio, July, 1960," held by the International Association of Universities. International Universities Bureau. Paris, 1961.
153. Elvin, Lionel. "Education and Technical Assistance: The Technical Ideas," *Journal of Education* (London), LXXXIX (1957), 376-78.
154. Folkman, William S. "Rural Problem Areas Need Better Schools," *Agricultural Economics Research,* XIII (October, 1961), 122-30.
155. Furnivall, J. S. *Educational Progress in Southeast Asia.* New York: Institute for Pacific Relations, 1943.
156. Halsey, A. H., Jean Floud, and C. Arnold Anderson. *Education, Economy and Society.* New York: The Free Press of Glencoe, 1961.
157. Harbison, Fredrick, and Ibrahim A. Ibrahim. *Human Resources for Egyptian Enterprise.* New York: McGraw-Hill Book Company, Inc., 1958.

158. Henry, Nelson B., ed. *Social Forces Influencing American Education,* Part II. (National Society for the Study of Education Yearbooks, No. 60.) Chicago: University of Chicago Press, 1961.
159. Hill, F. F. "Scientific Manpower for the Less-Developed Countries," *Annals of the American Academy of Political and Social Science,* 331 (1960), 26-31.
160. Hoselitz, B. F. "Non-Economic Barriers to Economic Development," *Economic Development and Cultural Change,* I (March, 1952), 8-22.
161. International Bank for Reconstruction and Development. *The Economic Development of Nicaragua.* Baltimore: The Johns Hopkins Press, 1953.
162. Kahl, Joseph A. "Three Types of Mexican Industrial Workers," *Economic Development and Cultural Change,* VIII (January, 1960), 164-169.
163. Kellogg, Charles E. "Transfer of Basic Skills of Food Production," *Annals of the American Academy of Political and Social Science,* CCCXXXI (September, 1960), 32-38.
164. Kerr, Clark, John T. Dunlop, Frederick H. Harbison, and Charles A. Myers. *Industrialism and Industrial Man.* Cambridge: Harvard University Press, 1960.
165. Keyfitz, W. "The Interlocking of Social and Economic Factors in Asian Development," *Canadian Journal of Economics and Political Science,* XXV (February, 1959), 34-46.
166. Moore, Wilbert E. *Industrialization and Labor; Social Aspects of Economic Development.* Ithaca: Cornell University Press, 1951.
167. ― "Labor Attitudes Toward Industrialization in Underdeveloped Countries," *American Economic Review,* VL (May, 1955), 156-65.
168. Mosher, Arthur T. *Technical Co-operation in Latin-American Agriculture.* Chicago: University of Chicago Press, 1956.
169. Myint, H. "An Interpretation of Economic Backwardness," in *The Economics of Underdevelopment,* eds. A. N. Agarwala and S. P. Singh. Bombay, New York: Indian Branch, Oxford University Press, 1958.
170. National Manpower Council. *Womanpower.* New York: Co-

lumbia University Press, 1957.
171. Nicholls, William H. "Accommodating Economic Change in Underdeveloped Countries," *American Economic Review,* XLIX (May, 1959), 156-68.
172. Read, Margaret. *Education and Social Change in Tropical Areas.* London and New York: T. Nelson, 1955.
173. Redfield, Robert. *Peasant Society and Culture; an Anthropological Approach to Civilization.* Chicago: University of Chicago Press, 1956.
174. Schultz, Theodore W. "Agriculture and the Application of Knowledge," in *A Look to the Future,* pp. 54-78. Battle Creek: W. K. Kellogg Foundation, 1956.
175. — *The Economic Test in Latin America.* (Cornell University, New York State School of Industrial and Labor Relations Bulletin, No. 35.) Ithaca, 1956.
176. Shearer, John C. *High-Level Manpower in Overseas Subsidiaries; Experience in Brazil and Mexico.* Princeton, New Jersey: Department of Economics and Sociology, Industrial Relations Section, Princeton University, 1960.
177. Shils, Edward B. "Intellectuals, Public Opinion and Economic Development," *World Politics,* X (January, 1958), pp. 232-55.
178. Svennilson, Ingvar (University of Stockholm). "The Transfer of Industrial Know-How to Less Developed Countries." April, 1960. (Mimeographed.)
179. Tang, Anthony M. *Economic Development of the Southern Piedmont, 1860-1950.* Chapel Hill: University of North Carolina Press, 1958.
180. United Nations. Department of Economic Affairs. *Measures for the Economic Development of Under Developed Countries.* A Report by a Group of Experts Appointed by the Secretary-General of the United Nations. New York: United Nations Department of Economic Affairs, 1951.
181. Vakil, C., and P. Brahmanand. "Technical Knowledge and Managerial Capacity as Limiting Factors on Industrial Expansion in Underdeveloped Countries," *International Social Science Bulletin,* VI (No. 2, 1954), 212-17.
182. *Vocational Training for Rural Youth.* A Statement by the

NPA Agricultural Committee, September, 1960. (National Planning Association Special Report No. 58.) Washington.
183. Westermarck, N. "The Human Factor and Economic Progress," *Indian Journal of Agricultural Economics,* XVI (April-June, 1961).
184. Zolotas, X. *Economic Development and Technical Education.* (Bank of Greece, Papers and Lectures, No. 4.) Athens, 1960.
185. Youngson, A. J. *Possibilities of Economic Progress.* New York: Cambridge University Press, 1959.
186. Yudelman, Montague. "Some Issues in Agricultural Development in Iraq," *Journal of Farm Economics,* XL (February, 1958).

V. General or Unclassified

187. Anderson, C. Arnold. "A Skeptical Note on the Relation of Vertical Mobility to Education," *American Journal of Sociology,* LXVI, No. 6 (May, 1961), 560-70.
188. Anderson, C. Arnold, and Philip J. Foster. *Discrimination in Education.* Chicago: University of Chicago, Comparative Education Center, 1960. Mimeographed.
189. Benson, Charles S. *The Economics of Public Education.* Boston: Houghton Mifflin Company, 1961.
190. Blitz, Rudolph C. "Algunas caracteristicas educacionales de edad e ingreso de la fuerza de trabajo en Santiago y Valparáiso," *Instituto de Economía.* University of Chile, forthcoming.
191. ―― "Some Classical Economists and Their Views on the Economics of Education." A lecture given at Johns Hopkins University, April 3, 1958. Mimeographed. Also published in Spanish: "Algunos economistas clasicos y sus opiniones acerca de la educación," *Economía,* 72-73 (1961), 34-60. (Universidad de Chile).
192. Bone, Louis W. *Secondary Education in the Guianas.* Chicago: University of Chicago, Comparative Education Center, 1962. Comparative Education Series, No. 2. In press.
193. Bowman, Mary Jean. "Jobs and People," to appear as part

of a forthcoming book, *Resources and People*, by Resources for the Future. Baltimore, Johns Hopkins University Press.

194. Conant, James B. *The American High School Today*. Carnegie Series in American Education. New York: McGraw-Hill, 1959.

195. —— *Slums and Suburbs: A Commentary on Schools in Metropolitan Areas*. New York: McGraw-Hill, 1961, 1st edition.

196. Coombs, Philip H. "The Technical Frontiers of Education." The Twenty-seventh Annual Sir John Adams Lecture at the University of California at Los Angeles, delivered March 15, 1960.

197. Correa, Hector. *The Economics of Human Resources*. Den Haag, Holland: 1962.

198. David, Martin, Harvey Brazer, James Morgan, and Wilber Cohen. *Educational Achievement — Its Causes and Effects*. University of Michigan, Survey Research Center Monographs, No. 23. Ann Arbor, Michigan, 1961.

199. "The Economics of Indian Education," *Capital*, Supplement of December 22, 1960, pp. 11-16.

200. Elkan, Susan. "Primary School Leaves in Uganda," *Comparative Education Review*, 4 (2) (1960), 102-9.

201. Elvin, Lionel. "Educational Development: Some Economic and Social Considerations." Based on an address given to the sectional meeting of the National Union of Teachers on January 4, 1961.

202. Fisher, Irving. *The Nature of Capital and Income*. New York and London: Macmillan Company, 1906.

203. —— *The Theory of Interest*. New York: Macmillan Company, 1930.

204. Floud, J. E., A. H. Halsey, and F. M. Martin. *Social Class and Educational Opportunity*. London, Heinemann, 1957.

205. Foster, Philip J. *The Transfer of Educational Institutions: The Ghanaian Case Study*. A Ph. D. dissertation, University of Chicago, 1962. Microfilms available.

206. Harris, Seymour E. Economics of Higher Education. New York: Harper and Brothers, 1960.

207. Harris, Seymour E., ed. "Higher Education in the United

States: The Economic Problems," *Review of Economics and Statistics* (supplement), XLII (August, 1960).

208. Kahan, Arcadius. "The Economics of Vocational Training in the U.S.S.R.," *Comparative Education Review,* 4(2) (1960), 75-83.

209. Karol, Alexander G. *Soviet Education for Science and Technology.* Cambridge: Technology Press of Massachusetts Institute of Technology, 1957.

210. Keezer, Dexter M., ed. *Financing Higher Education, 1960-70.* New York: McGraw-Hill Book Company, Inc., 1959.

211. Kristensen, Thorkil, and Associates. *The Economic Balance.* Copenhagen: Munksgaard, 1960.

212. Machlup, Fritz. *The Production and Distribution of Knowledge in the United States.* Princeton: Princeton University Press. 1962.

213. Ministry of Education. *15 to 18.* Vol. II. A Report of the Central Advisory Council for Education — England. London: Her Majesty's Stationery Office, 1960.

214. Organisation for Economic Co-Operation and Development. Summary Report and Speeches by Dean Rusk, Thorkil Kristensen, Philip H. Coombs, and Walter H. Heller, at the *Policy Conference on Economic Growth and Investment in Education,* Washington, D. C., October 16-20, 1961. Paris, 1962. (See also under II-B above.)

215. Petty, Sir William. "Political Arithmetic," *The Economic Writings of Sir William Petty,* ed. C. H. Hull, Vol. I, pp. 233-313. Cambridge: University Press, 1899.

216. Riesman, David. "Education and Exploitation," *The School Review* (Chicago), 1960, pp. 23-35.

217. Rivlin, Alice M. "Research in the Economics of Higher Education: Progress and Problems," in *The Economics of Higher Education,* ed. Selma J. Mushkin. Washington: U. S. Department of Health, Education, and Welfare, Office of Education, 1962.

218. Rockefeller Brothers Fund. "The Pursuit of Excellence," *Education and the Future of America.* (Rockefeller Report on Education, Special Studies Project Report, V.) New York: Doubleday, 1958.

219. Stephenson, Richard M. "Stratification, Education and Occupational Orientation," *British Journal of Sociology,* 9 (March, 1958), 42-52.
220. Tawney, R. H. *Some Thoughts on the Economics of Public Education.* (L. T. Hobhouse Memorial Lectures, No. 8.) London: Oxford University Press, 1938.
221. von Thunen, H. *Der isolierte Staat,* 3d, ed., Vol. 2, Pt. 2, pp. 140-52, 1875. Translated by B. F. Hoselitz, reproduced by the Comparative Education Center, University of Chicago.
222. Vaizey, John. *The Economics of Education.* London: Faber and Faber, 1961.

INDEX

Japan, 69
Job: information, 53, 65; opportunities, 22, 40, 65

Knowledge, production of, 4, 52, 67

Land-grant colleges and universities, 15, 46
Loans, for schooling, 22, 31, 69

McGuffey Reader, 18
Man power, high level, 42
Mexico, 28–30, 60, 69
Migration, and schooling, 40, 53
Moral purposes of education, 3, 8

National income, 8
National Science Foundation, 39
Nigeria, 41–42

On the job training, 30, 53, 54, 58, 65, 66
Opportunity costs, 6, 20, 23, 66; in time of students, 27–32
Overinvestment, incentive to, 22

Parochial schools, 21, 37, 66
Poor countries, 6, 31, 59, 60, 69
Producer capacity, 10, 58
Professions, independent, 53
Public policy, and education, 14–19

Rate of return, on educational investment, 10, 22, 43, 45, 54, 56, 58–63, 64
Research: agricultural, 39, 46, in hybrid corn, returns, 39; basic, 16, 17, size of staff, 39, cost, 39; educational, growth from, 46
Resources: allocation of, 2, 12, 18, 23, 42, 55; human, 10, 41, 42

Salaries, see Wages and salaries
Scholarships, 6, 18, 23, 30, 66
School attendance, 33; of farm children, 6, 30, 66

Schooling: by defense establishment, 35, 36; satisfaction from, 8, 38; scope of, 4, 35, 65; years of, 44, 48, 50, concept, 3, cost, 33; see also Colleges; Elementary schools; High schools; Parochial schools; Vocational education
Schools: as firms, 4, 12; transformation of, 14, 15
Science and technology, 7, 14, 17, 28
Scotland, 27
Soviet Union, 25, 28, 69
Stability, economic, 11, 12, 14, 18, 19
Supply price, of educational factors, 13, 32–35
Sweden, 69

Talent, discovery of, 4, 40; see also Children, talented
Taste and preferences, influenced by education, 3, 8, 57
Tax: exemptions, 36; laws, 31, 37, 65, 66, 69
Teachers: instruction, 4, 41; salaries, 9, 35
Techniques, new, in education, 13
Training, job, see On the job training
Transfer payments, 23, 52, 65

Uncertainties, economic, 22
Underinvestment, 56–58
Unemployment, 18
United States, 6, 7, 9, 11, 12, 14, 24, 25, 28, 29, 32–34, 43–46, 49, 52, 59, 60, 62, 63, 67
University: functions of, 4, 27; research, 4, 20, 52

Venezuela, 29–30, 61
Vocational education, 14, 18, 35

Wages and salaries, 11, 52, 65; of white and non-white workers, 53
Wealth, material, compared with educational wealth, 51